Botto

by

Christopher Gillett

To:
Lucy, Tessa and Adam

ISBN: 9781797790725

Hors d'oeuvre

If you were to threaten me with a stick of liquorice and ask me if I am a fan of a particular school of philosophy, I'd have to say Absurdist. You would have to be a very evil person though, because liquorice is the devil's work. Beelzebub's candy.

Why Absurdist? Partly because I've been a fan of Albert Camus since I studied French at school, and have always fancied the whole thing of hanging around in cafes drinking coffee, smoking Gitanes and sneering at the world. But mostly I'm an Absurdist because I do think our existence is essentially absurd and we try to give it meaning by looking for meaning.

Of course you're quite welcome to disagree. I have no problem with that. Just write your own book.

Now, I'm not going to claim that I have written three Bottom books as a philosophical treatise. That would be hilarious. No. But if life is an absurd thing, being a jobbing opera tenor is even more so. What a ridiculous thing to do. So, if it's about anything at all, this book - like the other two - is about doing a completely ridiculous thing and looking for meaning.

All the Bottom books have been about me telling bits of my story, interspersed with other reflections on the opera business, and some other things too. I tell my personal story not because it's a story that needs to be told for posterity. I tell it because I hope it will entertain. This is one of the reasons these books rarely follow a chronology.

If I think you're going to get bored by hearing about my upbringing, I skip to something else. Quite often I just want to get something off my chest. Sometimes I put in a date and a place and sometimes, when it doesn't matter, I don't. I'm not trying to piss off historians.

This book certainly isn't about someone overcoming his difficult background to make an enormous impact on the world. Sorry, there's not a lot of struggle in this book. Not much I can do about that I'm afraid. But what my story does have going for it is that some of it is quite odd.

Some material has been published elsewhere - in *Opernwelt* and in Linda Kitchen's *Opera Lives* - and revised for this book.

Spotted Dick

London, 1983

"Who told you to punch Constant's hair like that?"

Huh? I can't quite hear the question. The auditorium is big and unfamiliar. The stage too. There are strong lights in my eyes. I feel hot even though it's not hot.

"Sorry?" I say.

"Who told you to pronounce Constanze like that?" says again the voice in the stalls.

Ah. They've found me out.

I hadn't planned to sing Belmonte's aria at all. I don't really like the aria and I didn't spend any time preparing it for today. I don't even want to sing the role as even at my age - I'm 24 - I can tell that Belmonte is a bit of a bore. Prudish. Virtuous. Where's the fun in virtue?

No, I was planning to sing another aria altogether, Macduff's aria from *Macbeth,* which I've rehearsed with the pianist and which I've prepared pretty well. But the tenor before me, Kim Begley, has just sung that. He wasn't supposed to sing it. I don't know what he was supposed to sing but it wasn't the Verdi. It was all agreed yesterday, at the National Opera Studio. They arranged the audition for English National Opera. We couldn't be in the Coliseum, ENO's normal theatre, because of some rehearsal or other, so we're at the Theatre Royal, Drury Lane. It's a lovely, lovely theatre, no doubt about that. I wonder if I've ever been here before, as a child perhaps, to see a panto or Peter Pan.

5

I was supposed to sing the Verdi and Kim, one of the other two tenors at the National Opera Studio that year, was supposed to sing something else. That was the plan. Perhaps he was supposed to sing Belmonte? But I've turned up at Drury Lane, lovely theatre, just as Kim is singing *my* aria and I've been told I should sing something else. *How about Belmonte?*

What on earth possessed me to pronounce Constanze like that?

I had ridden to the audition on my moped and as I got inside the theatre and took off my crash helmet, I could hear Kim over the backstage tannoy, doing his audition. He was in the middle of the little cadenza at the end of Macduff's aria. *What the fuck?!* He sounded good, the bastard. Much heftier than my version, probably because his voice is heftier full stop. But I like to think mine has an italianate quality that will surprise and please the audition panel. What I lack in heft, I can make up for in style, I tell myself.

Well that's all down the toilet now isn't it? I've quickly mugged up my Mozart backstage and I've come onstage and in my nerves and unwelcome sense of panic, I've sung the opening phrase "Constanze, Constanze..." with the bizarrest of vowels on the final "e". It's more like an "o" with an umlaut. All closed and dark, when it should be open and bright. It seemed like a good idea at the time. It seemed safer to do that than sound all nervy and out of control.

"Constanzö, Constanzö..."

So who was it in the auditorium who asked me why I sang it like that? The Big Three are out there in the stalls: David Pountney, Peter Jonas and Mark Elder. I've auditioned for ENO before but only in an open audition where a minion is assigned the task of separating the wheat from the chaff. As far as I know, I've never sung for this lot, though it's not impossible that one or two of them might have heard me in one of the shows I've done at Sadler's Wells in the last couple of years. It's anybody's guess.

I think it was Pountney. He has a bit of a reputation. Him and his big sideburns and flamboyant trousers. From the way he's asked the question "Who told you to pronounce Constanze like that?" it is clear that they too have had their *what the fuck* moment, probably sniggering a bit, making faces like I'm a waiter who's just asked them if they want HP Sauce with their lobster.

What do I say? I don't know why I pronounced Constanze like that. I have no idea. Certainly no-one actually told me to pronounce it like that because I haven't worked on the aria with anyone at the Studio in recent memory. I can't simply admit that I was woefully unprepared to sing the thing in the first place and that they're lucky I've remembered *any* of the words. I could forget ever working for ENO if I said that.

"Constanzö, Constanzö…"

I really do feel hot.

"Um. No-one told me NOT to pronounce it like that" is what I say.

I think I hear a snort of laughter.

Oh well done, Gillett, now they not only think you sing like an idiot, but you've made it quite clear that you haven't a clue what you're doing unless someone else tells you what to do.

A long, hot pause.

"Thank you" another voice says.

I slink off stage.

It takes me another five years to be employed by English National Opera, but I've never worked with Pountney or Elder, who, I assume, still remember me as the twat who couldn't pronounce Constanze. They surely must have thought about it every single day ever since, Christmases and their birthdays included, because they have absolutely nothing better to do with their lives than remember a duff audition I did thirty-four years ago. I mean, if I can remember it so clearly, surely so can they. It stands to reason. Doesn't it?

Rum Baba

While many people recall their childhood as a succession of romps through sunlit meadows accompanied by a large, loving dog, many of my strongest memories take place inside a Wimpy Bar. It's a Wimpy Bar across the Brompton Road from Harrods, mind you, but a Wimpy Bar nonetheless. And it's in Knightsbridge. (American readers, imagine there is a Denny's on Manhattan's Park Avenue and you'll get the picture.) Wimpy Bars are Britain's chain of crap burger bars before McDonald's crosses the Atlantic in the 1970s. The tables are formica-topped, the food comes on plates, the ketchup in big plastic squeezy tomatoes.

Of course, Knightsbridge in the 1960s isn't the Knightsbridge it will become. For a start, middle-class families like mine live there, as opposed to the mega rich oligarchs who will own but rarely visit its real estate in the future. In her later years my mother tries to assert that we are upper-class "whether you like it or not", but I've met many people from the upper classes and I'm sure I'm not one of them. Upper middle-class, perhaps, but not upper-class. My father drives a second-hand Ford Zephyr and I never have a nanny, so I think that settles it. On the other hand our furniture is all dark brown and old, the rugs are Persian but threadbare and torn, the lumpy sofa is dotted with cigarette burns, so my mother may have a point. Not buying furniture because you are already well-supplied with crumbling old stuff is surely a tenet of the British upper class. It's possible I may be posher than I think.

In the early 1950s my grandparents bought a very small house for my parents as a wedding present, in a street so small it was omitted from the pocket A-to-Z, Fairholt Street. Not bad for a wedding present though. It cost my grandfather, Harold, a shrewd, kindly accountant and shellshocked survivor of the Somme, £5,000. That was about one year of his wages in 1950, at an educated guess. So, quite spectacular for a wedding present in fact. The house was a reluctant gift, as Harold suspected his son Robin was profligate with money, lazy even, inclined to spend without the foresight to invest.

Robin was an only child and routinely spoiled by his mother, Audrey, who doted on him and gave him everything he wanted, including a high opinion of himself and the keys to his new home whether her husband Harold liked it or not.

My father was an only child because his mother found childbirth painful and disgusting, refusing thereafter to have sex with my grandfather for the rest of her life. It's quite possible that my grandfather, whom I adored rather stereotypically, turned to the services of the many call-girls that worked in Shepherd Market in nearby Mayfair. Certainly, I remember my father telling me that his father seemed to be on first name terms with several women in the area, though I've never got to the bottom of how my father discovered that. I have my suspicions. As a younger man with a rosy-spectacled view of my grandfather, I preferred an interpretation that the women knew Harold from his many good works rather than because he was paying them for the nookie he couldn't get at home. As an older man, I am less inclined to judge.

I didn't like grandmother Audrey very much at all. She was cold and boney. And I wasn't alone. My mother claimed she was widely known as The Witch. Of the hundreds of photographs we have of her, she is smiling in almost none. At my christening she looks like I've just shat on her spindly lap.

Audrey didn't go to my parents' wedding in Paisley, near Glasgow, such was her disapproval of my mother whose father, John Findlay, another kindly man who at the time owned a steel foundry, she considered to be "in trade" and therefore entirely NOT what she had in mind for her darling boy, my father.

I say my mother's father was kindly, but I only gather that from photographs, in which he is always beaming. I cannot remember him or his wife. She died before I was born and he shortly after.

The Witch was the first person I can remember dying, when I was a small boy. I remember thinking I should be more upset than I actually felt. We were in Frinton-on-Sea at the time, a bastion of middle-class respectability, where we spent every Easter and summer holidays and where my grandfather had captained the Home Guard. After I was told the bad news I got on my stubby little bicycle with its training wheels still bolted to the back axle, pedalled off along the pavement and did my best to feel sad.

I hope my grandfather quickly took the opportunity of his recent widowerhood to roger himself silly in Shepherd Market but I'll never know.

The Wimpy opposite Harrods is where my older brother Nicholas and I are sent when my parents go out for the evening.

My father works in the City, which in the 1960s means wearing a uniform of short-jacket morning suit every day. He carries an umbrella and wears a bowler hat. He has a mundane office job in admin at a firm of insurance underwriters. If a burglar alarm goes off at the weekend, it's my father who has to drive to the office and sort it out. If somebody has to be hired or fired, I think that's his job too. I'm really not sure what he does all day. His is a generation that "does something in the City" and who don't go to work so much as "go to the office". That's all I know.

Two newspapers are delivered in the morning, *The Times* and *The Daily Express*, and after work my father brings home *The Evening Standard* or *The Evening News*. My mother is the avid reader of the papers, cutting out recipes and sticking them in neat scrapbooks, scanning the gossip columns for tattle. We take *The Daily Express* because her uncle is a journalist on the paper. He is known in the family as Wicked Uncle Peter but he isn't so much wicked as a bit of a lad, as journalists are wont to be; the first man I hear being described as "a bachelor" with a mock-shocked tone of voice that suggests it is unlikely he will ever settle down. He'd rather drive fast cars and spend long hours in the pub or at night-clubs with his latest girlfriend. Wicked Uncle Peter shared a flat during the 50s with Robert Robinson, later to become the quizmaster on *Call My Bluff.* Not that

that makes any difference at all to my life except that Robinson is often on the telly and in the 1960s that counts for a lot.

London is very boozy in the 1960s. There are pubs on every corner, reeking of smoke and Watney's Red Barrel. Beer is advertised as life-transforming. "A Double-Diamond Works Wonders!" "Guinness Is Good For You!" One of my regular errands is to run to the local off-licence for a refill of the soda syphon which sits permanently on the sideboard, ready for a squirt into a scotch. Friends of my parents drink tankards of Black Velvet - a cocktail of champagne and Guinness - on Sunday mornings or bring straw-wrapped bottles of Chianti to glug with my mother's Spaghetti Bolognese. The pasta, bohemian in the 1960s, is bought in yard-long blue-paper packets from a local deli, The Capri Stores, where salamis and cheeses hang from the ceiling and where they also stock Bird's custard powder and Ribena, the necks of the bottles wrapped in tin foil. A lot of my childhood is spent being around people who get very pissed then drive home.

Every evening, my father returns from the office, drops the evening paper on the dining room table, heads to the drinks cabinet and fixes himself a gin and Dubonnet. He is a pipe-smoker, particularly and extravagantly when behind the wheel of the Ford Zephyr. My brother and I have a tendency to catch bronchitis. It will become a lifelong weakness, and I'm pretty sure this is due to the hours we spend closeted - unharnessed by seat-belts of course - in the back of the car while our father puffs his way through a few ounces of Balkan Sobranie. He keeps his tobacco in a yellow, oilcloth pouch, tucked inside a jacket pocket. The smell of my father, his clothing, his car, is tobacco and pipe-smoke.

My mother has had a classic well-to-do upbringing. Brought up in Scotland, she was sent to Cheltenham Ladies College then a finishing school and hoteliery academy in Switzerland. She is an accomplished cook and once had ambitions of opening a country house hotel long before they were commonplace. But all that has to be subsumed when she marries my father. Her job now is to be a wife and mother.

I barely see my father for the first two years of my life. For my brother, it is five years.

Leaving school in 1943, my father had joined the merchant navy, which he left in 1960 when he was Staff Commander on *The Empress of Britain,* a Canadian Pacific liner which plied back and forth across the Atlantic to Canada or cruised the West Indies. On one of these cruises he got to know George Formby, who bought my father terrible novelty souvenirs, a telephone with a handpiece that looked like a banana, that sort of thing. But it wasn't a friendship that continued ashore.

I grow up with this explanation for my father leaving the sea: the next step would have been a captaincy of a liner that could soon be scrapped, forced out of business by the move to transatlantic flying. And he wanted to spend more time with his family.

This is certainly the version he chooses for his autobiography. But the truth is he has an affair with a passenger - probably one of several, it seems, during his time on liners - who becomes pregnant. There is a miscarriage and the affair ends. My mother presents him with an ultimatum which makes giving up seafaring for a life in the City the easiest choice. She doesn't want her family to be subject of one of the gossip columns she is so fond of reading. [1]

But on dry land he is no better, even going so far as to set up a small flat with a mistress. Sent away to boarding school at the age of seven, I am unaware of what is going on at home, especially as my mother decamps to Frinton-on-Sea with her two sons for most of the school holidays. My father joins us at weekends after a week in the office, and in his mistress's arms too no doubt. There must be frostiness in Frinton, though I can't say I am particularly aware of it.

Much of this comes out thirty years later when I ring my parents and tell them my marriage is in crisis because I'd been having an affair. My mother says "exactly the same thing happened to us and I swore that if it happened to you, I would make your father confess the whole thing." Whereupon she hands the phone to him and he mumbles his way through as little detail as possible. I can almost hear him sweating. I'm not sure what is more interesting and shocking, that he's been unfaithful when he's never

---

[1] I recently found photographs of my father with one of his girlfriends in a box marked "Phew!"

struck me before as the type, or that she has been holding this over him for so long, waiting for the day to have her moment of revenge. Certainly, the alcoholism that has blighted the last fifteen years of her life suddenly seems to make sense.

Wimpy is the eatery-cum-babysitter of choice because it takes Luncheon Vouchers. My father is given Luncheon Vouchers as part of his salary. They are a common City perk in the 60s and 70s and he always seems to have several spare books of them, each wrapped in a sleeve of greaseproof paper. A £1 book of vouchers is enough to feed Nicholas and me at the Wimpy Bar. We can order a burger each, with chips, and a pudding (Rum Baba or a Knickerbocker Glory probably) to follow. As inflation takes hold in the 70s, the vouchers buy less and less. Still we are handed just one book and told to nip off to the Wimpy Bar, and gradually have to either forsake the pudding or supplement the cost of our dinner with our pocket money.

My brother leaves for boarding school, so I go to the Wimpy Bar on my own and still burger prices continue to rise. I'm going through a growth spurt and a small Wimpy meal, even coated with all the ketchup a big plastic tomato can dispense, no longer satisfies my hunger. I complain to my parents that they either have to give me more Luncheon Vouchers or just give me money to eat, and the trips to Wimpy seem to come to an end.

Cheese and pickle

Here I am, writing a book, more precisely editing the second draft, when Remembrance Day comes along. It's the centenary of The Armistice. I pull some old photo albums off a shelf, as I have done several times before. These albums were my grandmother's, my father's mother, the one that was known as The Witch. I realise I've only ever glanced through them and admired in passing her hand-painted illustrations, the photos of her and her friends as they volunteered as Red Cross orderlies in her home town of Lichfield. There's my posh grandma, which she tags as "self", scrubbing floors, knitting socks, caring for the wounded, British and Belgian. Hundreds of them. Most of the photographs are of wounded men, often in large, pram-like beds that have been wheeled outside for fresh air. The albums are riddled with little poems written by ordinary soldiers. Some of the poems are in French, and there are patriotic ballads, trench songs, salutations to the King... The albums are extraordinary.

A third album reveals a different story through photos and press cuttings. In 1935 my grandfather offers his wife a string of pearls for Christmas. She says she would rather he bought for her a plot of land between Frinton-on-Sea and Walton-on-the-Naze. She wants to build some good houses for low-rent tenants; social housing, if you will. She designs the houses herself, three bedrooms in each with all the mod-cons, and an architect polishes her drawings into proper blueprints. There are no shortcuts. These are good houses. She employs only local builders and they erect ten

17

units in brick and tile, with two houses per building. She lays the very first brick and visits the site nearly every day. At Christmas she throws a dinner at a hotel for everyone involved in the project, all ninety of them. Christmas pudding is served and there are crackers, says the local paper. When the houses are finished she charges just fifteen shillings per week in rent for each home, a third of which covers council rates. That's about £49 in today's money, only £32 of it actual rent. It's an extraordinary act of philanthropy.

The houses are still there today, "Audries" - her name was Audrey - and apart from new windows and a few minor alterations they look as they did eighty years ago. I think they were all sold off to tenants, but when and by who I have no idea. My normal guess would be that my dad inherited them and frittered them away, given his track record.

How this all squares with grandmother Audrey Gillett deserving the nickname of The Witch is a bit of a mystery. I can guess that her experiences during the war made her feel it was easier to heap benefits on the less fortunate through good acts than it was to show physical affection to her family. Or I can also guess that she was compelled by a lingering, pre-war sense of patronage; that this is what the upper-classes did. It was their duty. As she had "done her bit" during the Great War, so she would continue to do her bit in peace, before the next war arrived. These guesses are perfectly plausible but I've no way of finding out, and just when I thought I had everyone pinned in place - who she was, what she was like - something hoves into view that throws everything off kilter. It would be much easier for me to make sense of everything if my grandmother stuck to the role to which she had been assigned: cold, snooty bitch who doted on and spoiled my father. Easy. Straight out of central casting, the perfect part for a dramatic soprano whose career is on the wane. But oh no, she has to turn out to be all complex and interesting. Mezzo-soprano territory.

Brown Windsor Soup

The very last time I eat in a Wimpy is in the early 1980s. I'm singing Elgar's *The Dream of Gerontius* - a somewhat daft thing for someone who is 22 to be singing - for the Barts Hospital Choir. It's the usual thing: a rehearsal in the afternoon when you sing the whole piece followed by the performance when you sing it all over again. After the rehearsal my voice feels a little tired and husky, which is no surprise as Gerontius is a big sing. Along with the other soloists I go to a nearby Wimpy for a bite to eat before the show.

In the 1980s food is difficult to find at 5.30 in the afternoon. Nowhere is open between lunch and dinner except Chinese restaurants, Angus Steakhouses and Wimpy Bars. Sandwich bars close up after lunch. I have a Wimpy burger and chips, and to follow, a Brown Derby, which is basically a ring doughnut with a scoop of vanilla ice-cream and chocolate sauce on top.

A Brown Derby is everything that a neurotic singer shouldn't eat before a show but that night I sing like a dream. My voice feels clear and clarion, which is something of a surprise. Aged just twenty-two I think I have found the answer to the classic what-to-eat-before-a-show conundrum.

When you're on the choral society circuit what you eat before the show is not usually within your control. "Your fee for Tittingsbury Choral Society's performance of *Messiah* is £25 plus travel. Hospitality will be provided by a member of the society who will give you supper and a place to change." Hospitality is more commonly known as Hostility; supper, a cold plate of gelatinous packet ham and salad with nasty, acidic salad cream that has the consistency of house paint. "I know how you singers don't like to eat too much before you perform!" is the catchphrase of the unwitting hostess. The changing facilities are a child's bedroom, cold and long abandoned, the walls still decorated with My Little Pony wallpaper.

At another Gerontius a few years later, this time in Guildford Cathedral, the host is unusually obnoxious, showing off his large, vulgar, self-built house and bragging about his recent drive to the south of France in his Rolls-Royce. His building firm gives more money than he would like to the choral society in which his wife warbles and clearly he feels we are in his debt. Seeing my little Fiat Uno in his drive he says "I bet you could fit your car in the boot of mine." During the concert I spot him looking bored in the second row, just behind the mayor, and fix him with a you-can-fuck-the-fuck-off stare.

I often think about that Wimpy Brown Derby and its healing powers, especially when my voice is tired. Something else brown - soup - nearly causes my humiliation during another *Gerontius,* this time in Exeter Cathedral with David Willcocks conducting. After a morning rehearsal the soloists are given lunch in a nearby hotel. I choose the Brown Windsor Soup to start with. It's basically a strong beef soup. Innocuous, you would think. A

21

safe bet on a concert day. If we'd been in a Wimpy I would be saving room for a Brown Derby too.

As soon as I ingest the first spoonful of soup I can feel a strange gurgling in my stomach and a knot forming in my bowels. Uh oh. I get through the rest of lunch feeling queasy. The rest of the afternoon is spent on the lavatory cursing all things brown and cursing the hotel kitchen.

I try to nap, sweaty and anxious. No good. Imodium isn't yet a thing. The only over-the-counter remedy I knew for diarrhoea is kaolin and morphine, a disgusting medicine that only half works and which, yes, contains morphine. It isn't something you want to take before singing.

Come the evening, I pull on my tails then pull them off again to rush to the lavatory. This happens twice. The soloists gather in the cathedral vestry a few minutes before the concert and I wonder if I have enough time to go again. I don't. We mount the podium with Willcocks and take our bows. I sit down and the prelude begins. Memories swirl in my head of a story about a famous tenor who supposedly shat himself during a concert at the Royal Festival Hall. Am I about to suffer the same catastrophic humiliation in front of a full cathedral? More gurgling from my bowels. Sweat. How can I possibly survive the six-page prelude, let alone the whole first part? I rock lightly in my seat. Should I leave the podium and rush to the loo? I won't have time. And what would Willcocks think? He would have to stop. It would be all too embarrassing no matter what I do. My only hope is that the feeling building in my bowels is more wind than substance and that I can hold it in.

The prelude, gorgeous but interminable that night, concludes. I stand up. *Oh god oh god oh god.*

With a weak and wavery voice I start:

"Jesu Maria, I am near to death." *Never a truer word spoken.* My bowels continue to fill with something. *Please be air please be air please be air.*

"And thou, thou art calling me." *Hmm, a bit feeble that. You'll never get through this marathon role singing like that but oh whatever you do don't try supporting from too low…*

"I know it now. Not by the token of this faltering breath, this chill at heart, this dampness on my brow…" *You're telling me.*

"Jesu, have mercy! Mary, pray for me!" *You betcha.*

"Tis this new feeling, never felt before" *Aside from ALL afternoon that is.*

"Be with me, Lord, in my extremity!" *Less talk about extremities thank you.*

"That I am going" *YOU ARE KIDDING!*

"That I am no more. Tis this strange innermost abandonment, Lover of souls! Great God! I look to Thee." *And here comes the killer line…*

"This emptying out of each constituent" *You couldn't make it up…*

"And natural force"…*REALLY?…* "by which I come to be. Pray for me, O my friends; a visitant is knocking his dire summons at my door…" *That's one way of putting it…*

I keep this up for four pages and then suddenly, woosh, adrenalin, Dr Footlights or whatever you want to call it, rushes through me. I can actually feel it, like a warm tap being turned on. My bum closes like a terrified clam. The nausea and above all, the overwhelming urge to empty my bowels into my trousers vanishes as quickly as it arrived. Spared my utter humiliation I suddenly feel uncommonly positive. And that's pretty rare.

Fried Bread

1966

A month before my eighth birthday I am sent to join my brother Nicholas at Durlston Court Preparatory School, a boarding school on the Hampshire coast, about one hundred miles from home. It's not a notable school. It's just where my grandfather was sent when he was a boy. My father managed to avoid boarding school until he was thirteen.

The last few weeks at home have been spent getting me kitted out. Some of my school uniform I inherit from Nicholas, some of it is bought new. Pairs of grey serge shorts, long socks, sandals, a school blazer and cap, cricket boots; they are all packed into a trunk, my school number, 26, painted on the top. In my wooden tuck box go books, toys and a ration of sweets that is surrendered to Matron on the first day.

The trunk and tuck box are sent ahead, picked up from our house and taken by train in the goods van.

The holidays end with my mother cooking a special lunch of steak and chips, before we take a taxi to Waterloo Station. We never normally take taxis, only the tube or bus. We only take taxis when we are being sent away to school. The route is always the same, past the front of Buckingham Palace, across Westminster Bridge and into the station. From now on I will always think of being sent away to school when I eat steak and chips or cross Westminster Bridge, or take a taxi.

The school has reserved some compartments on the early afternoon train to New Milton. There are labels gummed to the carriage windows. Other boys in the same uniform are all already on board. Some wave to my brother. They've done this before. There aren't many new boys like me joining in the summer term. The station is noisy and smells of oil and smoke. I've barely ever been on a train until now. Trains in 1966 are still being pulled by steam engines.

My father joins us at the station. It's the end of his lunch hour and he's wearing his bowler hat. He has taken the tube - the Waterloo-City line or The Drain, as it is known - from his office in the City, bought a platform ticket for a couple of pennies and joined us by the train. He looks at his watch as if he hasn't got much time. We shake his hand, hug my mother and climb aboard.

The guard blows his whistle and the train pulls out. We won't see our parents again for another three weeks.

For the first three nights I wait for the dormitory lights to go out and then I cry quietly into my lumpy pillow. The bed frame is iron, the mattress stuffed with horsehair.

My mother writes twice a week; a page and a half on blue writing paper. She signs herself Mummie, not Mummy, as she doesn't want us to think of her as Tutankhamun. We write back at weekends, our letters scrutinised by one of the masters for signs of dissent or misery. Our parents need reassuring that they did the right thing. We don't tell them that we sometimes call Matron "mummy" by mistake.

After three weeks our parents drive down on a Saturday. They're staying the night in a hotel and after Nicholas and I have finished the day's schedule of lessons and sport, we drive there for afternoon tea. It is the first time we have left the school grounds since the beginning of term. It's forbidden otherwise. The rest of the world happens beyond the school gates but we have no place in it.

We come back to school in time for supper and bed. On Sunday we see our parents again. They come to matins in the school chapel and then we go out for Sunday lunch at their hotel, where the starters before the Sunday roast are either tomato juice with Worcestershire sauce, tomato soup, or a half grapefruit with a glacé cherry in its hub. Puddings come round on the sweet trolley: orange slices in syrup, chocolate mousse, trifle or jelly.

After an afternoon mucking around in the New Forest being careful not to get our uniforms dirty, we are driven back to school in time for "prep" (the boarding school equivalent of homework), when our parents will say goodbye and return to London.

As we drive back to the school my father lights his pipe and turns on the radio. It's time for *Sing Something Simple*, "a collection of favourite songs, old and new, sung by The Cliff Adams Singers, accompanied by Jack Emblow on piano accordion" on the BBC's Light Programme. It is unbelievably awful, mawkish and sentimental. It becomes the soundtrack of being taken back to school in a smoke-filled car and anticipating saying goodbye. From now on I won't be able even to think of the Cliff Adams singers accompanied by Jack Emblow on piano accordion without feeling sick.

After my parents have gone, and I've done my prep and the lights are out, I cry all over again.

The school food is terrible. We have a lot of fried bread, almost at every meal, and all we seem to get are the end crusts. I don't know what happens to the middle slices but we assume they are saved for the staff. The bread is deep fried until it is deep brown. At breakfast, when we might expect to eat toast and marmalade, we eat fried bread and marmalade. The fried bread, nothing but crust, is very difficult to eat. It's so hard. Rock hard. Too hard for soft young teeth. You have to stick it into the side of your mouth and attack it with your molars. If you try to cut it, you won't succeed. You have to stab it and if you do, it shatters into a hundred pieces, shrapnel flying across the room, sticky with shredless catering marmalade and slimy with grease.

Also on the menu, a lot, is deep-fried Spam in batter. It drips with fat. And there are baked beans. Vast vats of baked beans. I hate the Spam but hunger teaches me to like it. I work out that if you pile the baked beans onto the fried bread and leave them a short while, the tomatoey juice softens the fried bread. Then if you share a forkful of bean-and-fried-bread with a chunk of greasy Spam fritter and chew it all together, the taste of Spam gets masked by the tomato sauce.

Puddings are nearly always semolina or tapioca, with a gob of jam in the middle but never enough.

The sweets that have been sent with us to school are kept in biscuit tins in The Tuck Room, a store-room with a fold-down hatch. Twice a week we are allowed two small items from our tuck tin. Any tuck that's left over is handed over on the last day of school, when we sugar-binge and feel sick.

Reheated Leftovers

Aix-en-Provence, 2015

I have returned to Aix-en-Provence to sing yet again in a production I first did 24 years ago, Robert Carsen's now-famous *A Midsummer Night's Dream.* When we premiered it in 1991, Carsen was anything but famous. Only a few years before I'd worked with him at Glyndebourne. He was Trevor Nunn's assistant on *Idomeneo* and was in charge of all the cover rehearsals. As well as singing in the chorus I was understudying Idamante, so we spent a lot of time working together. Robert often used to wear a vivid blue jumpsuit and one of the Glyndebourne chorus wags nicknamed him Good Housekeeping.

The Aix *Dream* was arranged very late, on a very small budget, after a co-production which had bombed horribly at Sadler's Wells was dropped. There was a sense at the festival that we were a second thought, a filler, the poor relation compared to the more glamorous operas on offer that summer. We rehearsed in a hot, dusty, school gym on the outskirts of town and had very little time on stage. We were simply expected to fail, another festival production that's done once and never seen again.

And then we were suddenly a massive success, the toast of France. Europe, even. Robert's career took off like a rocket and the production travelled, returning to Aix this year for the first time since 1992, when we had been booked for an immediate revival, unprecedented in the history of Aix. In 1991 the cast had been ignored by the management. In

1992 we all had invitations to a champagne lunch by the festival director's pool.

I've done fifteen revivals of Robert's production over twenty years, all until now as Flute, the youthful Rustic who transforms into the inept but impassioned Thisbe in the play scene. My last time, at La Scala when I was 51, I could just get away with it, but now I'm 57, Robert finally decided my days playing a teenager were over. A Thisbe with varicose veins who grunted every time he got up from a chair was too much of a stretch. Fair enough. He asked me to do Snout, the Wall, instead. I was to be the only survivor from the original run.

Though Snout is a fun role - how often does one get to play a wall, an inanimate object? Surely the perfect part for a tenor![2] - I've missed young Flute. I've invested so much of myself into him and into the many gags I've added over the years. In fact, I've often thought that my career has exactly followed Flute's journey: the guy who wants to sing the handsome leading man but who ends up wearing a dress and playing the fool. He's basically me.

And now somebody else is singing Flute, my part. I'm not sure if I've felt mournful or jealous, probably both, but it's been very strange watching someone else be me.

--

Last night, I did a stupid thing; I watched myself on TV.

---

[2] We are so used to seeing inanimate objects brought to life, being anthropomorphised - thanks probably to Walt Disney - that we forget how extraordinary and inventive the idea would have been in Shakespeare's time, to have a man play a wall.

Nowadays it seems everything gets filmed and *A Midsummer Night's Dream* is no exception. I've given up trying to understand the contracts for these things. A TV contract used to be a big deal. It paid a lot of money, even though the opera was only shown once, on a less-than-popular channel, in only one country.

Now, it gets streamed all over the world, on the internet, into cinemas and public squares, and your fee might buy you a couple of Chinese takeaways. If it gets turned into a DVD you might be able to order some extra spring rolls. The contract even secures your rights "throughout the universe", just in case some TV executive thinks he might one day be able to sell your performance to the Klingons.

At home I have a pile of DVDs of operas I'm in and I've never watched them, simply because I hate seeing myself on screen. It's always disappointing. And I could do without more disappointment in my life.

So why did I slip and watch this broadcast?

As our more recent show was being streamed into homes across the globe, a lady in New York started tweeting at me during the performance, full of enthusiasm. I was flattered. Last night, a much-revered soprano messaged to me to say she was watching it on French TV. Again, lots of enthusiasm. Again, my ego was massaged.

I didn't even know it was on.

I thought I'd have a sneaky look... I got as far as my first scene.

It wasn't that it was bad. It's just that it was completely different to how I thought it looked and sounded. One little phrase, to my ears, sounded dreadful. What on earth was I doing with my face? This one performance, which I can do nothing to improve, is now recorded for everyone, including the Klingons. I can't take it back or say "let's do another take!"

I suppose the solution to this, in future, might be to film rehearsals and let us see what we're doing, to get us prepared. But, frankly, that sounds awful. No, my instinct is to keep opera where it should be, live for the audience that's in the theatre, where a passing disappointment can be forgotten and forgiven. But I suspect that's not going to happen.

One thousand year-old egg

Beijing 2016

Within twenty-four hours of our arrival in Beijing my phone was stolen. I would say "it's my own fault" but I haven't worked out yet why stealing something that belongs to someone else is anyone but the thief's responsibility. Let's put it this way: I was careless. The phone was in the back pocket of my jeans and in the push-and-shove of a subway train, someone nicked it.

Everyone in China has smartphones so why mine should be of any use to anyone I really can't say. It's not a fancy iPhone, it's a Chinese built OnePlus, and it's secured to the hilt with passwords and fingerprint recognition. As soon as I got back to the hotel, I wiped its contents remotely. While that's all very impressive, what I really wanted the phone to do was deliver a one-million volt shock to the bastard who stole it. Or it could play Russell Watson singing *Granada*, very loudly and unstoppably until the battery dies. That would do.

For some stupid reason, I imagined the Beijing subway to be as safe as the Tokyo subway when clearly it isn't. Either that, or it is just as safe but the contents of my bum pocket are just too tempting for a son or daughter of the Maoist state. Not that the phone has been much use in China anyway as half the things I normally do on it are banned and blocked. For the next two weeks I will be phone-free.

I'm in Beijing for two performances of *A Midsummer Night's Dream*. It's a revival of the production from Aix-en-

Provence, now into its 25th anniversary, and probably the Chinese premiere of the opera. Again I'm giving my Snout and, I hope, a great Wall in China.

The posters for the opera have a large photo from the production - a bed hanging in the air with Oberon and Puck in the foreground - and inset in one corner, a large photo of Carsen. I'm trying to remember the last time I saw an opera sold on the notion that a big photo of its director will get the punters in, and I can't. But then again I haven't been to mainland China before so I've no idea what floats their boat.

Like all good touring groups, the cast and production crew stick to a traditional routine. Every morning we arrive for breakfast just a few minutes before the restaurant closes and, having experimented once or twice with local dishes and decided we don't fancy them that much first thing in the morning, stuff our faces with as much western food as we can cram onto our plates in a single pass of the all-you-can-eat buffet. One morning, the breakfast room is crammed with a Chinese sporting team, clearly novices at the proper touring routine, given they got to breakfast early, and they've scoffed all the pastries. Bastards. One of them is eating her croissant with chopsticks, which in itself shouldn't disqualify her from having her *viennoiserie* but kind of does because, frankly, I fancied a croissant.

The hotel is new and mostly western in style. Its corridors are filled with the sound of Richard Clayderman, or someone of his magnificent talent, tinkling his way through "White Christmas", on a loop, twenty-four hours a day. It is

September. Perhaps it's Lang Lang. It wouldn't surprise me if somewhere in the hotel there was a live pianist locked in a cupboard, giving us the medley of his hit. I also suspect there's a man living in a hollow next to my hotel room whose sole job it is to monitor my internet use and keep me off forbidden sites like Twitter and Google Maps.

The hotel is a mile or two from the basketball court where we rehearse. We are picked up by bus for rehearsals and spend most of every commute at a standstill in gridlocked traffic. It would probably be quicker to walk. But walking comes with its own set of problems, not least of which is the smog. Some days it is so bad it even drifts into the hotel foyer where it hangs around the reception desk like dry ice at a Meatloaf concert.

Across the street from the hotel is a strip of shops and restaurants. I say street, but it's actually a six-lane road, permanently choked with traffic. The only way to cross is via a gloomy footbridge. Two of the shops are small supermarkets, one scruffy and cheap which we christen "Tescos", and the other up-market and expensive, which we call "Waitrose". This makes it easier for conversations like:

"Are you coming out to eat?"

"Nah, I think I'll grab something from Waitrose and eat in my room."

There's a restaurant nearby called Men Ding Li. A large banner over the entrance claims that its "meat patty explode the stomach". For some reason I can never find anyone who wants to go there for a meal. There's also a

McDonalds and by the time we are into stage rehearsals, many of us are slipping in for a quick burger rather than trying to navigate our way through another plate of noodles and unidentified fried objects. After a couple of weeks Andrew Shore, singing Quince, has abandoned Chinese food altogether. He's found a pizzeria he likes and takes himself there as often as he can. He can also get red wine there that isn't called *The Great Wall of China*, so he's a happy man.

We visit the Great Wall on a wet day. Soggy clouds swathe the hills. Visibility is so poor that we can only see a few hundred feet of the wall in any direction. The cheap ponchos we picked up in a little general store on the way cannot cope with large western bodies. They tear at the armpits and at the buttonholes, and a ceaseless drizzle makes its way into our socks and shoes. Still, the wall that would otherwise be so spectacular offers some diversions for an idiotic Englishman. One sign lists various phone numbers. One is for TELEPHONE CONSULTATION, another for RESCUE THE TELEPHONE. I could have done with that number back in Beijing.

The third is a COMPLAINTS HOTLINE and I'm left wondering what sort of person rings a hotline to complain about The Great Wall of China. Mongolians? Presumably there's someone manning the "hotline", but how often do they actually get to answer the phone? I suppose in England the equivalent would be a STONEHENGE COMPLAINTS HOTLINE, manned by a bloke from Wincanton who has to drive every day to a prefab office in Amesbury, make tea and wait for the phone to ring.

After an hour of pottering up and down the wall in the rain, I follow the sign that says THUS WENT DOWN THE MOUNTAIN and find my way back to our tour bus.

I do most of the big sights in Beijing, but once you've seen one bunch of old temples packed to the hilt with Chinese on holiday, you've seen them all. We're in the thick of several public holidays, so Beijing's attractions are stuffed. I visit the Forbidden City with Andrew Shore. My guide book gives details on how to get in and avoid the crowds. But it is out of date. You can't get in and avoid the crowds. You have to go in the main entrance like everybody without a Lonely Planet and show some photo ID to boot. Luckily I have my driving licence but Andrew has nothing on him. A stroppy ticket clerk yells something about him giving his licence number, so we just make one up and are admitted, all the while wondering if we are going to feel the gloved hand of a policeman plonked on our shoulder. Also I'm wondering if there's a FORBIDDEN CITY COMPLAINTS HOTLINE and whether it would be the same bloke who mans the GREAT WALL COMPLAINTS HOTLINE. The Forbidden City is impressive in its scale but I miss the human touch. I miss the National Trust and its kitchens and bedrooms. We wander around for a couple of hours, through squares and and gardens, poking into temples and galleries, but try as hard as I might, I can't imagine it as it must have been, and I feel guilty about my lack of enthusiasm.

Our first performance of *A Midsummer Night's Dream* is a curious affair. We are told that there will be a slight delay to the start while some speeches are made. This turns out to be an award ceremony, at which Robert Carsen is named *International Opera Artist Of The Year*, or something like that. We can't really hear, sat as we are in our dressing rooms, all warmed up and ready to go but now faced with a half hour delay. We can hear bursts of speaking, first in English, then in Chinese, smatterings of applause, then Chinese translated into English, more applause. Quite how many in the audience are familiar with the canon of Robert's work is a moot point, but no doubt they appreciate being told how wonderful the show is they are about to see just before they actually see it.

The Chinese orchestra - many of whom seem to have a pretty low opinion of Britten's opera, particularly the double basses who often come in when they think they should come in rather than when the composer thinks it might be a good idea - does a reasonable job and the performance is greeted as warmly as any audience can while it is simultaneously holding up its smartphones and filming the curtain calls as it tries to applaud. This is the new normal, I guess, particularly in China where they worry less about visual rights. Well, rights all round. (Just outside the Apple Store I've seen mobs of men selling knock-off iPhones, complete with knock-off packaging, for a fraction of the price you'd pay inside the store a few feet away. Apple's security guards were doing nothing. What can they do? Some were even chatting to the hucksters like old friends.)

The show finishes after 11pm but there's a reception at a smart hotel, attendance compulsory, despite having a show to sing the very next day. The hotel is barely a half-mile away but a bus has been laid on to take the entire cast to the do and we've been told we *must* take the bus. They don't like it when you don't do what you're told.

Anyone who has been on a tour will know that there is little more frustrating than waiting for a bus to fill up with a large cast. Ours has over a dozen principals and sixteen choristers, most of whom have large amounts of make-up to clean off. It takes half an hour to fill the bus. Because of one-way systems and dual carriageways, we can only get to the reception by taking a long way round, about three miles by estimate, in thick traffic. The driver gets lost. Then no-one is quite certain of the name of the hotel. Eventually we pull up where somebody *thinks* the do should be and finally, at midnight, we tentatively make our way into the foyer of an extraordinarily plush hotel. There's nothing remotely Chinese about it. It's style could be described as *Gigantic Boutique.*

Of particular interest to the famished cast is the buffet, which is full of Western dishes of lamb chops, mashed potatoes, green vegetables... you name it, it's there. Not a noodle in sight. Or Chinese wine, hurrah. We fill our glasses with expensive, decadent western claret.

There are plenty of local dignitaries to whom we should probably be polite and make small-talk as best we can, but a) how did they get here so quickly? Not by bus, that's for sure. And b) fuck 'em. We hit the buffet like a plague of locusts. Acid reflux be damned, yes I will have another glass of claret. Big slab of chocolate cake? Make that two.

The whole thing, paid for by the KT Wong Foundation, sponsor of the tour - must cost an eye-watering amount. How it squares with communism I have no idea. On the evidence of what I've seen, there is no communism, just rampant commercial capitalism with a lack of democracy thrown in for good measure.

A bit pissed and burping lamb and chocolate, we head back to our hotel at almost two in the morning. It's only a short, fifteen-minute walk and the streets, rather than being empty and silent, are absolutely hopping. There's an impromptu dance going on in the corner of a small park. Vendors have set up barbecues selling long skewers of grilled chicken. It could be Leeds on any Saturday night. It's not what I expected at all.

Peking Duck

I was heading to Tian'anmen Square, not because there's anything there I particularly wanted to look at, but because it's huge, hugely symbolic and a place where you can still witness the forces of authoritarianism at work. It's where you are most likely to find triumphant statues celebrating Mao and the revolution, and although you'll find Starbucks and KFC at the very fringes of the square, it's one of the few places left that don't seem to have succumbed to the ugly trappings of Western consumerism that have engulfed most of Beijing. I thought a bit of retro communist propaganda might be fun.

The square is absolutely huge - it will hold a million people easily - but I never got in. Imagine saying that of Trafalgar Square, a miniscule fraction of the size. "I got there, but I couldn't get in."

I took the subway to its southern end, left the station, followed signs down into another underground passage and up again, a pointless diversion if there was ever one, and followed yet another sign that led me to a security barrier. I had walked several hundred meters but travelled a handful.

They have security barriers everywhere in Beijing. You have to scan your bags to enter any subway station. I'm not sure what the exact threat is, aside from those pesky democrats, but on the subway trains the police run strange cartoons, animated *a la* South Park, warning of dark forces at work. Apparently, bad men, usually blonde and tattooed, will drive around shooting you if you fail to be vigilant. I think. Either that or it's a Chinese knock-off of *Team America*.

At the square, I approached the barrier. A small official barred my way and indicated that I had to join the back of a Chinese guided tour party, even though I wasn't part of the tour. The party filtered through in front of me, but when I got to the front, the same official barred the way again, putting his hand on my chest. He snapped something at me in Chinese. I said I didn't understand. He pointed into the distance and said, sharply, "one hundred meter!" So I said "oh fuck off, you can keep your stupid square" and loped off, muttering darkly to myself; an incident no doubt recorded by one of the zillion CCTV cameras that watch the area.

It was while I was fuming and muttering that I noticed the Beijing Railway Museum. I'd seen it listed on a map, but noticed that it wasn't mentioned at all in my *Lonely Planet Guide*. This could mean only one thing: it was a crap museum.

Now I rather like a crap museum. There's something endearing about wandering around a place that someone passionately believes should exist, but which in fact appeals only to a very, very small number of people. So, not unlike an opera house in fact.

Local history museums are the perfect example, especially the ones with a volunteer or two dressed up in period costume, using biros sticky-taped to pigeon feathers as "quills" and sporting comfy sneakers with their pilgrim garb. They never have enough money in the cash box to make change and the exhibition highlight is a display case full of bits of rock. Information on the exhibits is typed on curling sheets of paper that are gummed to coloured cardboard and stuck to the wall with BluTack.

I've been to crap museums all over the globe. The last one I went to, in Milwaukee, was so crap that the young student who was on the desk waived me in without charge, such was her surprise at seeing anyone at all. I was the only visitor. All day, probably. But I love being the only person in a museum, just as long as no-one bothers me while I'm there by asking me where I'm from and would I like to become a Friend of the crap museum.

Railway museums are usually very popular, especially if there are lots of working trains to clamber over and a good supply in the neighbourhood of stout, beardy men with a far-off look in their eyes. I had a hunch this museum wouldn't be one of them. I'm not sure if train enthusiasm is even a thing over here. Beards certainly aren't. And I was right. It was almost empty, probably due to the fact that it is a railway museum as opposed to a train museum. There really aren't any trains at all, just lots of displays about railway lines. And points. And signalling.

It was kind-of perfect, the displays so mind-numbingly dull that I could have a good giggle and almost forgive the officious little prick of a policeman in the square outside.

There was a captivating display of railway sleepers throughout history. That was next to another that showed the evolution of the things that clamp the rails to the sleepers. And don't get me started on the rails themselves or I'll be here all day.

One cabinet showed me a locomotive signal display and a signal junction box. They looked like bits from the insides of a washing machine so I'm glad I didn't miss those. And in a large display case all of their own, reclining on several square meters of red velvet, lay the modest pair of scissors that were used by Hu Jintao to open a railway line.

The basement was given over to large model landscapes of railway lines, impressive in their way but largely meaningless to me. When I approached the model of a Tibetan branch system, one of the museum attendants (of which there were many, all bored off their tits) nipped over to throw on a switch to illuminate in red the most important line in the model. It was the moment to deliver my payback for the Tian'anmen Square Incident, so I looked at it for about three seconds before walking purposefully away, hoping to convey that I wasn't much impressed.

People's Republic of China, 1 - Gillett, 1.

Moments later, I exited through a dusty gift shop. All I can tell you about Chinese railways is that they built a lot of them and continue to do so. Oh, and the first Chinese train was a knock-off and it was called The Rocket.

Some things never change.

Wild Boar

As usual, programmes were offered to the cast after *A Midsummer Night's Dream*, but I took a brief look at one of them and threw mine away. The main reason I didn't want a souvenir was that I already have enough programmes at home, boxes of them in fact, mouldering in our dark, damp attic. Why add yet something else to the massive piles of junk that my kids will have to take to the dump when I die? I don't see a queue of biographers lining up to chronicle my career (nor should I), so who needs them, apart from my ego? I'll confess here that I never understand people who keep shelves and shelves of books that they have already read but have no intention of reading again. What's the point? To show off?

The other reason I discarded the offered souvenir of our Chinese tour is that I glanced through the artist biographies, including my own, and was overcome with a deep sense of weariness. Let's face it, there can be nothing, ever, anywhere, printed on glossy paper that is more boring and ludicrous than a singer's biography in an opera programme. I'm not sure who they're supposed to impress, because surely "desperately trying to impress" can be the only motivation for the dreary prose, the endless lists of roles sung, the conductors sung with, the role debuts made... Mine is awful and I find it deeply embarrassing. It's like the dullest shopping list ever composed and I can't imagine anyone making their way through it, let alone a Chinese punter in the Poly Theatre, Beijing.

What's alarming is that singers rarely get frustrated by the lack of good writing in their biographies but get monumentally pissed off when someone gets some tiny detail wrong. "Agh, I didn't sing Ferrando in Rouen. It was in Rennes! It's a catastrophe!"

My simple response to that would have to be: "Who, apart from you, gives a shit?"

And let's not dwell too long on the headshots on which thousands of euros were spent to make each singer look exactly like each other: a dreary parade of big hair and goatee beards, desperately trying to project an image of ARTISTRY. My headshot is a selfie. I often argue with my agent that if casting directors are now making decisions based solely on fancy photos, we are all in deep trouble.

I've spoken to quite a few ordinary opera-goers who not only never read artist biographies but barely look at the cast list. Most of them assume that whoever is on stage deserves to be there and that's all they need to know thank you very much.

Hopefully, the artist biography will soon be a thing of the past. It can't be that long before opera programmes just list the cast and next to each name a QR code, one of those little boxes filled with dots of different shapes and sizes. The punter, if he really wants to find out more about, say, the Third Jew in *Salome*, will simply point his smartphone at the code and then be instantly directed to the artist's website, where he can browse his way through all the lists of roles, extravagant claims ("Britain's best-loved baritone" is an old favourite), and moody photographs he can possibly digest.

It would spare the world millions and millions of pages of unread glossy paper. Just think what that would do for the environment and the mental health of thousands of egocentric singers. Please, please, let's do it now.

Corned Beef Hash

Something novel happened to me the other day. I was rehearsing for an opera house who sent me an email from their marketing department, which said "We hope you're looking forward to sharing your experiences and letting your friends, family, professional contacts, colleagues, everybody know what you're working on!" They asked me to download their "personalized banners" for Twitter, Facebook and even email, all to advertise their show. They wanted me to subscribe to their YouTube channel, to use their Twitter hashtag and "join the conversation". In fact, there was very little they didn't want me to do.

I thought about it for about five seconds and then did none of it.

Now, I'm no stranger to social media. I get how it works. What I particularly do know about social media is that there is nothing more irritating than colleagues who do little else but go on and on about their career. "Thrilled and honored to announce I'll be singing Scarpia in 2016-17 for Utah Opera!" "Wow, you must come and see our *Madame Butterfly* and our awesome cast! Such a privilege to be a part of this amazing team!!" These are just two of the most common yet dullest of the genre and ones to which I take particular exception. The second would make me avoid a show with the same vigour as I'd avoid a rat with herpes. Apart from the fact I'm not sure there is *any* direct correlation between the excitement a performer feels about his job and the enjoyment of the audience - we are professionals after all, and the difference between us and amateurs is that we have to deliver the goods even when singing is the absolute last thing we feel excited about - I simply don't buy it.

More honest would be: "I can't believe it, someone actually gave me some work!" and "I'm in an opera and the chances are it might be quite good, but the chances are equal that it might be awful. I just hope we don't screw it up." Now that's a show I'd see.

I don't expect a lawyer to tweet how thrilled he is to be defending Billy Chopper, the Chorleywood Axe Murderer, any more than he should share his excitement at being booked by Colin and Doreen Haggis to do the conveyancing on the bungalow they're buying in Weymouth. If Billy Chopper gets handed down a life sentence, I doubt anyone would say of the lawyer: "his defence was pretty good, but where he fell short was that he simply wasn't excited enough." So, I hope no-one ever says of a singer: "her Elvira was really excellent, but I just wished she'd let me know beforehand that she was thrilled to be singing it, because that would have made it even better. I'm not sure how, but I really think it would."

So the idea of an opera company actively asking to participate in this sort of breathless bullshit is deeply depressing. Is that the best they can come up with? Do they really think that me tweeting "hey everybody, stop what you're doing and let me tell you how the show I'm in is so much better than the one you're in" is going to have people rushing to the box office?

I also dislike the implication that it's now my job to sell the show, to put bums on seats. I thought my job was to sing and act, to provide a quality product that sold itself. I didn't become an opera singer as a massive ego trip. Singing isn't an exercise in narcissism - well it shouldn't be - so why would you expect me to fill my emails and social media with advertising which is all about me? I'm not a pop singer, I'm an opera singer. I've got better things to do than self-promotion, like watching television and eating pasta, to name but two. And now that opera companies expect their employees to stay "on message" with their marketing departments - it's spelled out in our contracts that we must - I simply don't trust promotional tweets, any more than I would trust tweets put out by L'Oreal that 95% of all women actually believe there's "active anti-aging technology" in a face cream.

I'm not stupid. I do understand the the need to help out our opera companies. And of course singers, particularly the young ones, need to plug their work, but haven't we reached Peak Promotion Point already? Haven't we run out of hyperbole with which to sell our performances? Can't we be more imaginative than repeating the same old tropes about being thrilled and excited? If absolutely everyone is screaming "THIS IS THE BEST THING YOU WILL EVER SEE I PROMISE PLEASE BUY TICKETS OR I SWEAR I'LL SHOOT MYSELF!!!" what's the point in PR any more?

It's no surprise that agents now urge their clients to have an "active social media presence" in order to promote their careers. Needless to say, I mostly use my account to be an idiot or to lambast Donald Trump and fans of Brexit. Not that they take any notice. I've discovered that one agent is even charging clients £350 per month for "social media marketing advice". I can't help but wonder what it would be like if the great performers of fifty years ago lived and worked in today's world:

Hi, Mr Fischer-Dieskau! Can I call you Dietrich? Well, me and the guys in the office were just looking at your latest tweet and I think it could do with some pepping up. Here's what you posted: "Tonight I will be singing Winterreise *at the Konzerthaus, accompanied by Gerald Moore." Teeny bit dull isn't it? Next time, why not try to give it more happy thoughts?! More excitement?! And I'm not sure everyone knows who wrote* Winterreise*! I know I didn't until I Googled it! My bad! But do think of your young followers! And who's Gerald Moore? Is he with our agency? Don't think so! Best, Trixi xx*

(Junior Intern, Digital Marketing)

--

Dear D, I hope Schumann's Winterreise *went great! (See? That extra little info is sooooo useful!) BTW I played your record of it last night. Amaaazing. But you sound so sad and so serious! Haha just kidding! Anyway, following on from my last email, why not try something like this for your next tweet?: "Can't believe I'm singing Handel's* Creation *tonight with the bad boys of the Vienna Phil and my old mate Herbert von K! So excited! Can't wait! #lovemyjob"*

What do you think? I really think this will get some bums on seats and fill the hall. And it will really score with the younger audience too. Kisses, T xxx

--

Dear Dieti (the girls in the office had a vote and this is what we're calling you now! LOL!), I didn't realise that the Creation *concert was already a sell-out. Congrats! I must say I'm surprised, given I didn't see much on Twitter about it. (Are you sure it's by Haydn? We sang it at school a couple of years ago and I could have sworn it was by Handel. Craaazy piece!) You must feel like quite the star! Wooohoo! Though it would have been great if you could have got a photo after the gig. Best of all: a selfie with you and Herby von K goofing around backstage! That would have been so much fun! Or in a restaurant, partying hard. I know what you guys get up to! Anyway, we've made great progress and I think this is going to give your career a fab boost. Keep it up! Next step is to get you tweeting photos of your breakfasts. Ooh, and airports. I think people will find it really interesting. Keep this up and I think you'll get thousands of Twitter followers and your online profile will really take off!*

Glad to help! Hugs, Txxxx

P.S. Herby von K is sooooooo handsome! OMG his hair is gorgeous! Xx

Chicken a l'Italiana

"So, Dave, what do you do?"

"I work for British Rail, Chris. Signalling."

"Really? Interesting."

"Yes, it is quite interesting, Chris. But I don't get to meet a lot of members of the, um, fairer sex in the signalling world, Chris. That's why I come on 18-30 Club holidays. To be honest you see, I won't lie, I'm looking for romance, Chris. This is my fourth 18-30 so far. No luck yet though, I'm afraid. But, keep it to yourself…" Dave moves in closer. "I'm actually 34."

Dave looks about 36. His hair is thinning. He habitually wears long shorts, dark socks and sandals.

We are in a seafront bar in Cefalu, in Sicily. It is a Friday night, the end of the first week of a fortnight's package holiday. It's supposed to be a party, but I'm stuck in a corner with Dave.

I've never been on a package holiday before. A couple of months ago I decided I needed a holiday. I'm only twenty-three and not adventurous, self-confident or happy enough in my own company to head abroad entirely on my own. Besides it's the early 1980s. Travel abroad means visits to travel agents, printed timetables, guide books, maps… It's so much easier for the inexperienced holidaymaker like me to pick up an armful of glossy brochures and go from there.

It's clear from the brochures that if I go on holiday in September, the only time I can manage in my surprisingly busy singing schedule, I will either have to holiday with a lot of very old people on a Thomas Cook package or I can take the 18-30 Club route. The 18-30 Club brochure verges on soft porn and it all looks pretty exhausting - the endless FUN and PARTYING - but Cefalu looks less terrifying than what appears to go on at the Costa Brava, so I hand over a cheque and hope for the best. I have no girlfriend, no attachments, so who knows, I might even get lucky. Dave and I are not so very different.

When I check in for my charter flight at Gatwick I'm alarmed to find the queue brim full of old people, all with Thomas Cook labels on their luggage. It's only when we land in Sicily and are met by Jen, our 18-30 Club rep, a large but effervescent woman, her voice knackered by late nights, booze and cigarettes, that I and my fellow clubbers are corralled into an identifiable group of not-old people. The brochure had rather given the impression that the flight would be full to bust with the young and beautiful. Where are they all?

It turns out there are eleven of us, ten men and one woman. The sole woman is on her honeymoon with one of the men. That leaves eight men plus Dave the overage signalman from British Rail in his socks and sandals. We board a bus to Cefalu, which we share with forty-odd elderly Thomas Cookers, destined for the same hotel. This isn't turning out at all how I expected.

The 18-30 Clubbers are invited to a Welcome Drink ("one FREE DRINK per clubber") to meet some Clubbers who are starting the second week of their holiday. As we arrive at the hotel bar, the rookies are given the traditional "fun-filled" greeting of being squirted with water pistols by the veterans. We look a bit pissed-off and their heart isn't in it, so it doesn't last long.

Jen, the enthusiastic rep, signs up those of us who want to go on outings - a fun meal here, a crazy disco there, a visit to Agrigento to see the amazing temples, a shopping trip to hopping Palermo - all of which she coaches in terms of being super-fun and exclusive to the Clubbers. When the outings happen, the bus fills up with more Thomas Cookers than Clubbers. Even for the disco.

The disco is outdoors, at another hotel. The Clubber's table is dominated by Steve, clearly the Alpha Male of the previous week's group. He exudes cool confidence, taking long drags from his cigarettes, dominating the table. The most attractive women of the holiday sit either side of him, vying for his man-juice.

Someone asks me what I do. Here we go.

"Opera singer."

Nothing. I might as well have said "Microbiologist".

"I do have an Equity card though."

"Ooh, really?" asks a girl. "Let's see."

I take the little rectangle of cardboard out of my wallet. She looks at it, doesn't know what to say, so I put it back and the conversation ends. This is going nowhere.

I end up talking to Andrew and Simon, two of the men in my week. They're old friends and, as it turns out, good amateur musicians. Andrew is a dentist who also plays the trumpet, and Simon plays the trombone when he's not working in a bank. We even discover that Simon was playing in a Verdi Requiem I sang a few months ago in Ely

Cathedral. Andrew wasn't playing in that but we do discover that he slept with a cousin of mine, a good amateur soprano, when she and he were medical students.

On the bus back to the hotel Andrew and Simon cajole me into singing something. I'm a bit pissed, so it's not hard. The tour rep hands me the bus microphone and I let rip with *O Sole Mio.* But it's not really *O Sole Mio,* it's the Wall's Ice Cream version, the one they've been using in adverts. I don't know the words but Andrew does so he feeds them to me like an opera prompter.

Just one Cornetto! Give it to meeee!
Delicious ice-creeeeeam, from Italeeeee!
The nut and chocolate dreeeam,
Give me Cornetto from Wa-haaaaaall's Ice Creeeeeeam!!

The passengers on the bus are pissed too, so it goes down pretty well, especially amongst the Thomas Cookers. Next time we're on a tour bus, the local guide wants more. "Where eeez da guy from da eighteeen to da thirtee wid da boootiful voice?" When you're twenty-three you don't know any better so I give them *Granada* as well as the hit *Cornetto.* The next time we're on the bus the tour guide ignores me.

On the trip to Agrigento I'm surprised to see the Alpha Male, Steve. Where did he find the time in his busy schedule of satisfying multiple women and posing by the pool? Are ancient temples really his thing? What with him being a racing driver, nightclub owner, fund manager, spy or whatever it is he does. We fall into conversation.

"So you're an opera singer then" he says, nodding a bit with pursed lips as if that's all he's got on the subject.

"Fraid so. And what do you do?"

"Well you know when you get a letter in the post and it has those little blue dots on the front? I put those on. Southampton sorting office."

He's a postman. So I nod a bit and purse my lips too.

I move away from Dave as he pauses in his tales of railway signalling and romantic woe, grab a plate and help myself from the buffet. It may be Italy but the food isn't very good. It doesn't strike me as particularly Italian but as I've only been to Italy twice before I'm no expert. It's food for young people who don't like foreign food. But I pile my plate with chicken drumsticks, chips and lasagne and I get another beer.

An hour later, I'm on the disco floor and I think a girl-who-works-for-an-estate-agent who I don't really fancy asks me if I'd like to join her and her friend for a walk on the beach, but the music is too loud and I'm feeling rather peculiar so I really can't concentrate on what she's saying. I make a face that says *I think I'm going to call it a night thank you very much if it's all the same to you.* I walk back to the hotel feeling even more peculiar and make it in time to my room to throw up in the loo. Next it's the other end.

I climb into bed, and then run back to the lavatory. This goes on all night. I have a fever too.

I re-emerge after forty-eight hours, hungry and dehydrated. "Salmonella, I reckon" says Andrew the dentist. "Probably the chicken."

While I've been in bed, the first week's lot of have gone back home and the newest batch has arrived. This amounts to two girls. One of them, a tapestry expert who works at Hampton Court, has only booked for one week, meaning that the other girl, who works in a shop, faces the prospect of being the only person on an 18-30 Club Holiday. Just her and the rep. The company persuades her to change her booking to just the one week.

Also while I've been ill, Andrew the dentist has started bonking Jen the rep. Each morning he appears at breakfast looking ashen and exhausted. "Never again" he says. And each night after several beers he goes back to her room. His friend Simon calls him a martyr to his groin.

King Prawn

1984

"Evening, Shirley!" says a trumpeter from the Kent Opera orchestra as he passes me in the corridor. I look bemused.

"Shirley. You know, Shirley what's-her-name, the girl in *Goldfinger*."

"Oh, OH! Yes, of course. Ha bloody ha!"

The trumpeter has a point. The opera is Tippett's *King Priam* and I'm Hermes, messenger of the gods. I'm naked except for a golden nappy and covered from head to toe, hair included, with gold make-up. Only the centre of my back is unpainted, not for any safety concerns but because the audience won't see it. Still, I've seen the movie many times, I've heard the folklore. I'm glad there's a bit they haven't painted gold.

It's a lengthy process to get me gilded. I stand on a sheet of plastic in my pants while two make-up women slosh a basecoat all over me, then they add extra glittery highlights. Kent Opera tours during the winter months, to some of the older theatres in Britain. Adequate heating is rare.

Also rare are adequate showers to take the gold off after the curtain has come down. It's a bloody show too. Lots of gore on lots of the cast and chorus.

In Brighton, at the Theatre Royal, there are a couple of baths on a top floor. No showers. I rush offstage after the curtain call, climb the stairs two at a time and secure a bathroom before anyone else. Still, the bath is already stained with stage blood. Someone got to clean up before the curtain calls. I turn on the tap and cold water comes from both taps no faster than a trickle. This bath will never fill, and even it does, it will be very cold. I've a train to catch back to London. So I give up on the bath and do my best to wash my hair in a basin and to take off as much as I can on my face and neck. I'll have to shower when I get home.

I do the best I can while moaning to nobody in particular that a lack of washing facilities must surely be against Equity rules. I dress then ride the train home entirely gold from the neck down, gobs of gold in my ears and under my chin.

It's worth it though. The show is terrific and a big hit.

Michael Tippett comes to the first night, in Canterbury. Waiting in the wings for his curtain call, he spots that a stage hand has altered the name painted large on the back of a flat, from *King Priam* to *King Prawn.* There's a moment of anxiety that Tippett will take offence about the retitling of his grand opera. Many would. But he points at it and whoops with laughter. "King PRAWN!! Oh that's very funny!"

The director is Nick Hyner, the conductor Roger Norrington. Most of my entrances are made from the flies, descending from the heavens. Halfway through Act One, out of view of the audience, upstage of some massive sliding doors, a tiny platform on the bottom of a pole is lowered from the fly tower. I step onto the platform, barely larger than my feet, and the stage manager, Jamie Hayes, runs a strap through the waistband of my gold nappy, which he fastens to the pole behind me. If I were to faint I'm not sure what good the strap would do. Chances are I would come clean out of the nappy and plummet to the stage forty feet beneath me, all gold except for an embarrassment of white pimply flesh and shrivelled scrotum. As someone who can barely sit in the circle of a theatre without feeling vertiginous, these aren't exactly my dream working conditions. Being high up inside buildings is not something I enjoy. My feet tingle. I feel as if at any moment, my body will propel me forwards into the abyss. I cannot look at the ceiling because all I can think is: *I am too close to the ceiling of this very tall space.* But I'm new in the profession so I certainly won't object to being hoisted up into the dark flies, waiting there while whole scenes play out beneath my dangling little platform, staring straight in front, looking neither up nor down, scenarios playing out in my head where a wire snaps and I become impaled on a spear… For some reason I keep remembering a production of *The Gondoliers* which I have recently done at Sadler's Wells.

I was playing Marco, one of the two gondoliers of the title, the other being Giuseppe. It was a revival. Marco was played before by Kim Begley, who used to do a spectacular cartwheel across the stage during the opening duet "We're called gondolieri". At our first rehearsal the revival director said to me:
"OK, Chris, this is where you do a cartwheel across the stage."

"But I can't do cartwheels. I don't know how."

The director pouted and said, his voice dripping with disdain: "Oh, well, Kim could."

"I know. But I can't."

The director turned to Martin, the baritone who was playing Giuseppe. "Martin, can you do a cartwheel?"

Martin replied: "Yeah, sure, no problem. I'll just mark it in for the moment if that's OK."

"Sure, thanks Martin." The director looked at me as if to say "See, that wasn't so difficult". I expected him to pin a Scout badge on Martin for *Doing Cartwheels*. And another for *Not Being Negative With The Director.*

I was a little surprised by this exchange, principally because I knew for a fact that Martin was a really crap dancer. He had two left feet. He was notorious for it. I'd been told that fairly recently, as Papageno in *The Magic Flute*, he was supposed to ride a bicycle on stage but they had to cut it because he didn't know how to ride a bike. And now he could do cartwheels?

The rehearsals progressed and every time we ran the *Gondolieri* duet in the studio, Martin would indicate with a rotating motion of his hand that this is where he would do the cartwheel. Never once did he actually *do* the cartwheel. He just shimmied across the stage doing the thing with the hands. Judging by the splendour of his hand motions, it would be something worth waiting for.

Eventually, a week before the show opened, we got on stage for the first time. We ran the duet. Again, Martin did his hand-waving shimmy for the cartwheel. We got to the end of the duet, which involved lots of running around and dancing, and Martin breathlessly announced: "Phew. I'm puffed. Actually, you know what? I think I'm going to cut the cartwheel if that's all the same to you." And the cartwheel, unseen until now, was never seen again.

Up in the flies, in the dark, nothing in front of me but wires and spotlights, thinking to myself *well at least I'm not like Martin,* I am clutching a plastic apple. It too is spray-painted gold. It terrifies me, only because I am convinced that one day I will drop it. Props and me, we don't do well together, be it the retractable dagger that doesn't retract, the rope that snaps, the cigarette case that won't open on the first night... I've suffered them all. The moment a prop fails to work, you are basically doomed. It's not your lucky night, despite all those cards and novelty giftettes from your colleagues wishing you *GOOD LUCK, DARLING xxx!* Sorry, but the good lucks simply didn't work. The moment a prop goes wrong you may as well give up the idea of singing well because tonight is simply not your night and there's nothing you can do about it. The gods are not on your side. Which is ironic, given I'm playing a god. Or demi-god at least. The only bits of me that aren't godlike are the fleshy patch on my back and the contents of my nappy.

In Act Three I am up in the flies even longer. I have a lovely aria, a hymn to music, which I sing on my perch, twelve feet in the air, alone, bathed in a spotlight. It's one of the quieter moments. In an otherwise brassy opera, I am accompanied only by a flute, a harp, and the occasional piano chord. It strikes me as interesting that it is during this quiet, inanimate section - the only movement onstage some elegant gestures that have been choreographed for my hands - that Roger Norrington in the pit becomes more animated than anywhere else during the entire evening, his arms flailing in vast arcs above his head, way above the top of the pit. But, conductors, eh? What are you going to do? After the aria - which ends with a pianissimo high A flat - I'm whisked back up into the flies, where I stay for the rest of the opera; another ten to fifteen minutes of swaying gently in the darkness, everyone giving it hell-for-leather on the stage below.

On the very last show I reach the gloomy flies as usual and prepare myself for the wait until the end of the performance. As I stare straight ahead I notice something descending from above, a foot or so right in front of me. It's a bucket. *Oh ha ha, a sick bucket. Stage management having a last show laugh.* But when the bucket comes to a stop at my waist height I see it's not a sick bucket at all. Inside is a bottle of champagne, a glass, some chocolates, a punnet of strawberries and a folded copy of *The Times.*

I hazard a glance down into the wings. The Kent Opera crew - wardrobe, make-up and stage management - are all down there giving me thumbs-up signs, egging me on to tuck into the goodies they have so thoughtfully laid on. I'm so touched I could cry. I am also such a butter-fingers that I dare not reach into the bucket and take anything out, particularly as the quick glance downwards has made me feel a bit wobbly. Rodney and Neil are right underneath me, playing out the climax of the opera. The last thing they need is a handful of strawberries plopping onto their head mid-scene. Or a bottle of champagne. It could mess with the whole denouement, hearing a voice from the gods hissing "sorry!"

I wait until the final blackout and grab a choccy before my rapid descent back to the stage for the curtain call. The crew finishes off the contents of the bucket.

I sing the role again in Athens, at the Herod Atticus amphitheatre, when the Royal Opera takes its production over for a couple of performances. John Dobson, who had been the very first tenor to sing the role of Paris in 1962, is The Young Guard. He's now 54.

There's no set as such, just the ruins of the ancient theatre with large arched doorways for entrances and exits. Mike Ashman, who has been landed the task of adapting Sam Wanamaker's Covent Garden production, lets me do pretty-much what I want; which turns out to be almost exactly what I did for Nick Hytner's Kent Opera production. Rodney McCann too, singing the title role, is doing exactly the same. I'm even encouraged to do the arm choreography I used to do on my little podium, even though now I'm standing bang in the middle of the stage rather than dangling from a pole, mid-air.

We rehearse in the mornings and at night. It is far too hot under the blazing July sun to work in the afternoon. The acoustics are perfect. It's a fantastic place to sing, and the morning we work on my aria, I can see Tippett sitting at the back of the auditorium with his companion Meirion Bowen, better known as Bill. I feel it goes rather well. At the end of the rehearsal, someone asks me if I could go and have a word with Tippett.

I clamber up the steep stones of the auditorium. Tippett seems a little agitated, which is surprising. On the couple of occasions I've met him he's been all smiles and bon-ami.

"My dear, it really is a hymn to music, d'you see? I need to feel you are connected to the earth and to this higher deity, music. Man and god, d'you see? How can we make this connection? I don't know, perhaps you could take the hands of the flautist and the harpist or something. That's all I really wanted to say."

Quite honestly, while I can just about understand what he's saying, I have no earthly idea how anything he said can be done on stage.

Back at the hotel I manage to have a quick word with Bill.

"So, was Michael unhappy with the way I did Hermes for Kent Opera?"

"Oh no, no no no. Don't worry about it."

But of course I do worry about it. Perhaps that's the reason that on the first night I completely forget a last-minute change of plan and come on stage through the wrong doorway, my follow-spot perfectly picking up a doorway with no-one in it, while I start singing bathed in deep shadow.

I meet Tippett several more times, but it always seems like it's the first. There's never any sense he recognises me from the last time but that could be due to his failing eyesight. After a performance of his *Songs of Dov* at the Queen Elizabeth Hall, he comes on stage - his usual routine, bounding up to the stage and then shuffling very slowly the moment he's in the limelight - and just says to me, beaming: "That's right, love, just belt it out!" and I have no idea how to take it.

In 1988 I jump in at a few days' notice to sing his huge and very difficult *The Mask of Time* with Sir Charles Groves and the Hallé. I'd got the call on a Monday night and the concert is on Saturday. Kim Begley was supposed to do it but he's ill. The only other tenor who knows it is Bob Tear and Bob doesn't want to do it so he suggests me. I'm due to do Tippett's *The Knot Garden* at Covent Garden in a few months so I guess I'm reckoned a good fit.

Charles Groves's son and agent Jonathan does all the footwork. "Ask them for a bloody big fee!" he says. A massive vocal score that must weigh two kilos and some tapes of the first performance are couriered to me the next day. I have a couple of hours' coaching on it from Chris Willis, a repetiteur at Covent Garden who is unusual in his passion for contemporary music. I'm in the middle of a run of *Parsifal* at the Royal Opera, with one show during the week. Luckily it doesn't clash with any Hallé rehearsals.

When I first meet Sir Charles it is for a quick skip-through before we join the full orchestra. I am still sight-reading, every turn of the page bringing something that looks novel, unfamiliar and really tricky. By the end of the orchestra rehearsal, things are starting to take shape, and two days later, at the final run, I'm pretty secure. The really difficult writing is for the chorus. This is the first attempt by an amateur choir and they're doing a fantastic job.

During the final run, I have one big glitch, early on. A percussionist is supposed to hit a nice clean e-flat on a xylophone and, on the same note, I sing a little unaccompanied phrase "the lover can see". But the percussionist, who like his fellow players is running around bashing everything bar the kitchen sink, hits a different note altogether; a b-flat I think. I don't have perfect pitch but I know the difference between an e-flat and a b-flat. They are as close together as raspberry jam and Marmite. I start on the note he plays and then, realising it's wrong, stop and say out loud "Oh, no, that's not right". Groves seems oblivious and carries on. It's a runthrough so it's the right thing to do.

At the end of the runthrough, Groves looks pleased and a little tired. He's in his seventies so fair enough. He's ready to send everyone off for lunch. "Any problems anyone?"

I pipe up. "Er, yes, just one little thing."

"Hang on, everyone." I could swear I can hear a collective groan from the orchestra.

I huddle with Groves. "I think the xylophone is playing the wrong note here..." and I point out where it had gone wrong.

"Ladies and gentlemen, let's just play from figure three. The tenor is having trouble hearing the note from the xylophone." Well, huh, that's not exactly the problem but alright, I get it, diplomacy and all that, I'll take the blame.

We run the section from the xylophone e-flat and this time the player hits the note as clear as a bell. Hardly surprising as he hasn't had to run to the instrument from the tubular bells he's just been clanging.

"How's that?" says Groves. "Could you hear that alright? Good, thank you everyone!" And that's it until the performance the next day.

The hall is packed and bristling with microphones for a Radio 3 broadcast. Figure three and my little unaccompanied passage is approaching. The chorus and orchestra are crescendoing madly, gongs crashing, drums blazing, brass wailing. Silence. The xylophonist arrives swiftly from the tubular bells, grabs a mallet (though it might as well be a rolling pin) and donks it down on the first note he can find. Or that's how it seems, for the note is nowhere near an e-flat. It's a mid-range *thunk,* possibly an a-flat, a full fifth too low. I take his note, fool that I am, and the option to stop and say again "Oh, no, that's not right" being unavailable to me in front of thousands of eager Tippett fans, I soldier on. The result is pure Mariah Carey as I try to navigate the pitch back to where I think it should be during the word "lover", which now comes out as "loaauuuuveeeeer". On the strength of this cosmic reworking alone I could be shoo-in to sing *The Star Spangled Banner* at any American sporting event.

Nine years later I sing Tippett's *A Child Of Our Time* in its Russian premiere, in St Petersburg. Our hotel is a converted river-cruise boat that has been sailed up the Neva and moored at a jetty. The rooms are tiny cabins, so small I practically have to go out into the corridor just to turn around. The performance is mostly remarkable for the chorus. They are professionals but for the first time in the many times I've performed it, I'm aware that they truly empathise with the text. Unlike choruses back home, the Russians have experienced lines like: "The cold deepens. The world descends into the icy waters." Middle-class and comfortably-off, I feel a bit of a fraud singing "I have no money for my bread" in front of them. When they sing "Tell old Pharaoh to let my people go" they blow the roof off, the basses adding huge, sonorous bottom Cs, an octave below those in the score. I swear some of them go down to the bottom F below that.

I manage to get hold of one of the posters for the concert, which is big and all in cyrillic. I think it will be a lovely memento for Tippett who is now into his nineties and too frail to go to concerts, particularly in chilly Russia. When I get home I roll it into a poster tube and send it to him care of his publishers in London, Schott. It's the least I can do. Within a year he has died.

Many months later I get a letter from Bill Bowen. He tells me that he has just been given the St Petersburg poster. They were clearing out the mailroom at Schott and found the poster tube gathering dust on a shelf, where it had been put out of the way. Tippett never received it. "Such a pity as he would have been very touched by it."

Cold cuts

I'm thinking about the expression "once bitten, twice shy" a lot at the moment, simply because I'm about to start rehearsals in an opera house where I had an annoying experience about twenty years ago. I won't say which opera house, but it's in Belgium. In Brussels. Right in the middle.

I'm not being fair of course. The experience I had wasn't terrible when compared to some of the real horrors in the world, like malaria, Donald Trump, or Gardeners' Question Time, and it happens all over the place. It's one of those experiences that some opera professionals blow off with a shrug, but which gets most singers, like me, into a lather.

I'm talking about cuts.

It's not that I don't like cuts. I absolutely love them. I am never more thrilled than when they tell me Basilio's and Marcellina's arias have been cut from *Le Nozze di Figaro*. Hallelujah! Why anyone wants to sing them, let alone make people sit through them, is one of the universe's greatest mysteries. I've heard of some tenors who will only sing Basilio if the aria is included, which can only count as a triumph of Narcissism over Reason.

The only cut I can remember hating is when an idiotic conductor decided to excise a couple of pages from the great chorus *Thanks be to God* in Mendelssohn's *Elijah*. He did it, he said, so that he wouldn't have to pay the orchestra overtime. It took five minutes of the rehearsal to explain how the cut would work and another ten to rehearse it until everybody got it right. It shaved about twenty seconds off the performance while simultaneously ruining one of oratorio's finest choruses. But the conductor was very pleased with himself, so that was all that mattered.

The thing that really exercises my passions is when the conductor and the director either a) know what the cuts are going to be, but no-one can be bothered to tell the cast in advance, or b) can't be bothered to decide in advance what needs to be cut and they want to make these decisions during the rehearsal process. It's not hard to see that either scenario creates a lot of unnecessary learning for the poor singer. There is little more annoying than memorising pages of music only to have them chucked in the bin.

My experience in the un-named Belgian opera house in the middle of Brussels was probably all-too-common. I was to sing in the altogether unknown and forgotten *La Stellidaura Vendicante* (by Provenzale, to save you looking it up). You can't go to a music shop and buy a copy, so vocal scores had to be provided by the theatre. Two months before we were to start rehearsing, no score had arrived. I pleaded for a score. "Oh, right, we'll mail you one." Two weeks later a photocopied score arrived, but when I went to study it, the junior librarian or intern in charge of the task had managed to photocopy only every other page. It was useless. Not only that, but the text was written by hand and often indecipherable. I rang again. "Oh, right, we'll mail you one." It was nearly Christmas. It took three weeks to arrive, and when I opened the score (now with only three weeks to study and memorise it), it was still indecipherable but extremely long. I must have had five acres of recitative and eight arias. I got to work, struggling to make out what I was supposed to be singing.

At the first rehearsal, I sang my first aria then launched into three pages of recitative. "No," said the conductor, "this passage is cut. Didn't you get the cuts? Let me see your score. No, this is the wrong score!"

I kind of hated the opera house in the middle of Brussels for a while after that. But I'm willing to forgive.

I start rehearsals there next week. The production is a revival. After asking them for over a month, I got a list of cuts last week.

--

"OK, Chris, now you lead Liz to the table, the other guys hold her down, you pull off her panties and Andrew rapes her", says the director in Brussels.

"What sort of panties are they? Will they come off easily?" I reply.

"She'll be wearing two pairs. The ones you remove and a pair underneath. It won't be a problem."

"Good. I really don't want to struggle with them."

"No, it will be easy. Right, let's do it."

Yet another opera rehearsal. Yet another rape scene. Yet another situation where the men in the opera do something unspeakable to the women in the opera. At least in this one, the violation is in the score, a vital part of the plot, but it does make one stop and ponder how casually we do this now.

I'd say of the last ten operas I've done, I've had to play many more deviants and perverts that "normal" characters. You could argue that that's just how opera is. If a character isn't simply pining in unrequited love for another, he's pulling off their clothes and slobbering all over them. And that rule works no matter which gender is grabbing your character's eye.

But I'm sure when we used to have to rehearse this stuff, there was a degree of preparation. Conversations were had, permission was sought. It was a gentle process because it was an unusual and sensitive issue, especially for the female victims.

Now, there's no hanging around. "This is a rape scene, and off you go." It has become mundane and not in the least bit shocking, for the performers at least. And I bet the only operatic rape victims who benefit these days from some advance warning are the male ones.

When audiences at Covent Garden booed during a rape scene in "William Tell" I reckon it wasn't because they were surprised and stunned. It was because, yet again, there was a women being violated and they were annoyed by another director trying to shock them.

I don't expect there'll be a change in this trend any time soon, but I'm singing in *Billy Budd* next year and I'm already wondering what the chances are that I'll be the one who has to wear two pairs of underpants.

--

A long time ago I heard a story about a soprano who was rehearsing as Fiordiligi in a revival of a production of *Cosi fan Tutte* that she had sung before. They were working on her big aria *Per Pieta* and she was sitting in a rowing machine, as the production dictated. The rehearsal stopped for a moment and the soprano asked the director: "I'm sorry, I've forgotten, why exactly am I singing this glorious aria in a rowing machine?"

"Because if you don't, there are twenty sopranos who will!" replied the director, icily.

Asked what she did next, the soprano said: "I rowed like fuck!"

I think of this story every time the question of nudity arises. It happened to me very recently. I was already down to my underpants - and there is hardly a role I do these days, even *Turandot,* where I'm not stripping down to my underpants - when the director, Deborah Warner, said: "Chris, my dear, what do we think about going the whole way?" Ah, clever use of we.

"By the whole way, you mean completely naked?" I replied.

Now, I'm willing to bet all the tea in China that every single reader of this book has seen a nude opera singer. As a profession, we've been taking our clothes off and swinging everything around for decades. There's certainly nothing novel about the experience, nor is it particularly shocking any more. In fact, I'll go so far as to say it's become a teeny bit dull or at best, unintentionally funny.

When Deborah asked me to go the whole hog, this was in the back of my mind as I formulated my response. But I didn't say "oh don't ask me to do that because it's rather boring." No, I said this: "Quite apart from the fact that I really don't want to show off my wrinkly old penis, I think the reason it's not a good idea is because, if I were sitting in the audience, I wouldn't be shocked for the character; I'd be asking myself how the director persuaded that middle-aged singer it would be a good idea to take off all of his clothes in front of 2000 people. And I would be wondering about the singer and what he's feeling about exposing himself in front of all those people. In other words I'd be thinking more about the process of putting on the production than following the narrative of the opera..." And no sooner had I said that, than Deborah said: "Ah, good point. No, that won't do, OK, forget it."

And that, *mes enfants,* is how you persuade a director to let you keep your clothes on without getting fired.

--

I went to see a new musical recently. It was awful. Absolutely terrible. It was poorly-constructed, it was too long, it was full of clichés, it was dull, it was very very bad. But a friend of ours was in it. So, naturally, we saw her after the show and told her what a wonderful evening we had just enjoyed.

The audience, which had spent the evening in a mild state of catatonia, had leapt to its feet at the curtain-calls, as audiences in musicals are wont to do these days, awarding the cast a standing ovation. As far as I could tell, with my arse planted firmly in my seat, the cast found this reassuring but bemusing. Bemusing because I'm willing to bet that every single one of them knew that they were in a turkey. Though, to be fair, no-one could possibly fault the cast for their dedication in performing such a pile of tosh, so perhaps they deserved all the applause that could be lavished upon them.

In the opera business, as much as the music-theatre business, you need to be good at telling lies. You have to do it all the time. People rarely want to hear the ugly truth.

"Darling you were wonderful!"

"No, I didn't hear anything wrong with your top C."

"You do sound as fresh as you did thirty years ago."

"Yes, Herr Intendant, I have sung the role before."

"No problem, Maestro, it's very clear. I'll follow you."

These are useful lies to memorise and use as necessary.

Indeed, telling the truth could be considered something of a failing, jarring at the wrong time. A long time ago I sang an obscure baroque opera in Liege, then again a few months later in Brussels. The stage director hadn't been happy with his Liege staging and had persuaded *La Monnaie* to improve it by paying for a completely new version for Brussels. At the first night party, *La Monnaie*'s intendant Bernard Foccroulle lifted his glass to toast the cast, who sat in expectation of the usual extravaganza of praise.

"Well," he said, frowning, "it was better than it was in Liege."

Sourdough loaf

As any opera singer will tell you, it's important to have something to do to keep you sane while you're away from home. Some knit, some watch a lot of sport, some paint... I used to paint, but since the restrictions on liquids in hand luggage, the packing of my kit has become too difficult. And besides, if you get carried away with it, you end up with a pile of paintings that, somehow, you have to get home again. Taking arty digital photographs has become a lot more appealing than lugging canvasses.

Having something creative to do away from the rehearsal room is a good release valve, since the "creative process" in rehearsal is too often anything but, for the singer at least. Commonly it is frustrating, confusing and stifling. Oh and let's not forget boring too. Making something of your own lets off the creative steam much better than simply obeying the instructions of an indifferent conductor or under-prepared director.

Aside from a bit of writing, I like to bake sourdough bread. In all honesty, it's probably the most genuinely creative thing I do. The first time I baked "on the road" I was working at Glyndebourne, staying in a tiny studio in someone's garden. Fresh from a baking course near Edinburgh, I brought all my equipment in the car: sourdough starters, digital scales, scrapers, tins, *bannetons* (proofing baskets), French slashing knife (a *lame*)... It was a lot of stuff.

It's important to use words like *banneton* and *lame* in baking circles. These are code words, *shibboleths* if you like, that show fellow bakers - hipster bakers in particular - that you know your stuff. Though once you start talking hydration and protein levels you're well into baking nerd territory and I glaze over faster than a Krispy Kreme on a Saturday morning. Like any hobby, there's always someone who wants to make you feel you're not quite doing it well enough. In breadmaking they usually have big beards and beanie hats.

I had to figure out how to keep up my baking without lugging around half a ton of equipment, especially when going abroad and I think I've finally cracked it. First to go were the scales. Bakers have managed perfectly well for centuries without measuring everything to the nearest gram. Experience and a lot of practice has now taught me what will produce a reasonable loaf, and if those loaves are not always showroom quality, they're never inedible. There's plenty of room for small mistakes. One is, after all, baking a loaf of bread, not creating the Holy Grail.

Also banished from my suitcase are the tins, *bannetons* and special knife, the *lame*. The last one was easy. A bread knife works really well instead. Or a bog-standard razor blade - the type that goes in a single blade, old-fashioned "safety razor". It is important to slash the surface of the dough before you bake so that the bread can expand properly while it's baking. If you don't it will certainly split open, or worse, become constricted.

Instead of scales, I use cups, which you find in most digs or can pick up for a couple of quid. Or you can use a teacup. I've found that as long as the proportions are right, you're OK. After a while you get used to the feel for a good dough and can add more water or flour as need be. And one teaspoon of salt for a small loaf does the trick.

The big challenge is proofing. Normally, you bung your dough in a special basket, cover it and let it rise before turning it out and baking it. It's a delicate process but produces a loaf with lovely, distinctive rings on the crust, and it's definitely the best way to do it. But it's not the only way. I've found you can make a good bread by proofing the dough in a mixing bowl. Then you turn it out very carefully, upside down, onto a floured surface like a fat pancake. This you fold in half with as little disturbance as possible, rather like an omelette, before sliding it onto a baking sheet, slashing and baking. For this you need a bit of nerve and a good plastic scraper, the only piece of kit I really have to take on my travels. That and a hotel shower-cap. Shower-caps are brilliant for covering bowls of all sizes and stopping dough from drying out.

You may be surprised (I certainly was) that sourdough bread - the proper stuff, not the fake loaves they often sell in supermarkets - contains no yeast. Or sugar or fat, or any of the other things they slip into bread these days. It rises through natural fermentation. So, all a sourdough loaf contains is flour, water and salt. That's it. The starter (or *mother* or *levain* if you're being particularly poncy) is flour and water that has already fermented, just by being in a warmish place for a while. A very small amount of it sets off a fermentation when you mix it with yet more flour and water. It's beautifully simple.

The biggest challenge has been packing my sourdough starters, both wheat and rye. Travelling to America, I worried that a tiny porridge of flour and water would throw US Customs into a tizz, guns un-holstered, "move away from the porridge, punk!" and all that malarkey, but the first time I tried to declare them they weren't interested. I even ticked the box on the customs form that said I was carrying food but they just waved me through.

Now, just to be safe, I put about a heaped teaspoon of gluey starter which I've thickened with extra flour into tiny make-up pots and pop them in my toiletries bag. Almost as soon as I've landed I nip to the nearest supermarket, buy some flour (and some tupperware pots if need be) and revive my little bubbling babies as soon as I can. So far I've had no failures, no dead starters on arrival.

My main pots of starter I keep at home in the fridge. When I go away for more than a couple of weeks they go in the freezer, where they'll sleep for months.

Both my starters, wheat and rye, have kept going until I first fermented them in 2014. On the breadmaking course, our instructor, Andrew Whitley, gave us each a gob of his rye starter to add to our own. Andrew studied baking while a student in Russia during the 1960s and he brought back home a small plug of thick starter hidden in one of his socks. His starter is still rooted in that starter, and that starter predates living memory. It could go back as far as Rasputin, or even Pushkin. What a legacy in a porridge of flour and water.

Cold baked beans

1971

Aged twelve, I am sent to Pangbourne College. It's an unlikely choice for a child of my emerging skills. I've been a decent treble in the school choir and I've sung Pitti-Sing in *The Mikado* and The Judge in *Trial by Jury.* I've progressed from being a good recorder player, winning some prizes at local festivals, to playing the clarinet. It's an instrument I don't remember wanting to play for any other reason than my older brother Nick plays it too, but I'm quite good at it, better than Nick, which is all the motivation I need to stick at it.

Pangbourne College has recently changed its name from The Nautical College Pangbourne. The name has changed but the style of the school less so. Originally conceived as a rival to Dartmouth College, which prepared teenagers for a career as an officer in the Royal Navy, Pangbourne does the same, but for the merchant navy.

The boys - it's an all-male school - look just like naval midshipmen. We dress as naval officers and we are called cadets in the Royal Naval Reserve. The day I roll up to Pangbourne in April 1971, I am Cadet C. Gillett RNR.

I'm at Pangbourne because my brother is already here and my father, who unlike his two sons actually wanted to join the merchant navy, was here during the war. The epitome of a "a minor public school", its academic reputation is terrible. Barely any of its graduates go on to university. Most become estate agents or get a job in the City thanks to their parents' connections. If it has a reputation, it is for sport and for being a place where "problem" boys are sent to have some discipline hammered into them. It's a school for the difficult and "the thick" who are lucky enough to have parents whose wealth can protect them from getting nowhere in the state system.

The regime is harsh, militaristic, as you might expect.

It's obviously the ideal place to send a twelve year-old boy who has reached Grade 5 playing Mozart on his clarinet and whose piping treble voice has not yet broken. Such is the paucity of Pangbourne's academic and artistic ambitions that they don't even offer a music scholarship. But, presented with the rare opportunity to educate a boy who might actually be good at something other than running around in a muddy field clutching a rugby ball, they invent one, a whopping £100 a year off the school bill that my grandfather is paying because my father can't afford it.

Marching is big at Pangbourne and we do a ton of it. There are two parades a day, one after breakfast, when we muster on the parade ground and the flag - the blue ensign - is raised, and again in the evening when it is lowered. On Sunday there is a big parade after chapel, complete with a marching band and armed guard. So, the first thing the new boys must do is to learn how to march. In the first two weeks we are drilled for hours. The insides of my cherubic thighs become raw and chafed as the rough serge of my new uniform trousers rubs constantly against them while we march back and forth non-stop. The parade ground at the heart of the school is treated as a sacred place and it can only be crossed by marching or "doubling", which is like marching and running at the very same time.

We also learn how to spit-and-polish our shoes, to polish brass, to clean our cap covers. Most of all I learn how not to be punished. I'm terrified of the punishments, which are meted out by the senior at boys, the Cadet Officers as they are called. They can send you on Akkers, when you have to run at dawn between the two ends of the school and back, followed by a cold shower. Or they can give you an Extra Parade if your uniform isn't up to snuff. Or extra cleaning tasks, known as Divisions. Or Extra Drill, where you run around the gym with a rifle held above your head. The list goes on and on. Only canings are left to the discretion of headmaster but I know of none while I'm there.

It's intimidating stuff for a twelve year-old and I want none of it.

The director of music has little enthusiasm for his job. And who can blame him? I sing in the choir, but we're a motley lot, only good for propping up the hymns. My clarinet teacher is a retired army bandsman. After a few terms he gives up for good and the director of music can't find a replacement. It can't be easy to persuade any peripatetic teachers to make the journey for so paltry a collection of students. This goes on for more than a year; the only music scholar in the school and I'm having no music lessons. Still, at least I'm building my nautical skills with three lessons of Seamanship a week and four of Navigation. I'm quite good at Navigation as it turns out, scoring an A in my O-level. I'm also rising through the ranks of the marching band, in which I play the fife; the bugle or drums being the only other options. The band's repertoire is learned entirely by ear, led by older cadets. Wrong notes are handed on from generation to generation, uncorrected by anyone with any musical authority.

When I'm fourteen, my voice still unbroken, the director of music makes a final stab at his job and puts on a performance of Britten's *Noye's Fludde*, which is also fourteen years old. I play Ham, arguably casting the mould for my future career. The chief excitement is that GIRLS have to be bussed in from Reading and I end up with my first GIRLFRIEND, Lorna Parcell, who is twelve and playing Mrs Ham. It's a good old-fashioned showmance. I have no idea how to speak to GIRLS, having no sisters and having been in all-boy schools since the age of five. We write letters to each other with SWALK written on the envelope and hold hands on the one occasion we get to meet outside school. She breaks it off after a month or so and I mope, heartbroken for a day or two.

The food at Pangbourne is awful. Dark brown curried mince sits on gluey rice and is made exotic and just about edible with sprinklings of diced banana and dessicated coconut. Liver is another menu regular and I learn to become adept at separating the flesh with its texture of drying plaster from the huge rubbery rings of artery that make up most of a portion.

There is no hot food on Saturday evenings. Instead, a buffet is laid out of under-ripe tomatoes, salad leaves, and wet ham. Finishing off the spread is a vat of cold baked beans. Most boys do what I do, make a couple of slices of toast and dollop the beans on top before the toast gets cold. Stirring mustard into the beans gives them an extra kick. Cold beans and mustard: A Pangbourne Salad.

On coach trips away from school we are given a packed lunch, handed to us in a small paper bag, which never waivers from the same formula: a packet of two cream crackers, a rectangle of cellophane-wrapped cheddar, a small pat of butter, a Wagon Wheel, and an apple. In five years at the school I never once succeed in solving the conundrum of loading cream crackers with butter and cheddar whilst on a moving coach. First, I'm lucky if the cream crackers are still in one piece in their packet. If they are, and I can get them out of the plastic wrapper without them shattering, I am now holding two crackers in one hand while trying to open the foil-wrapped pat of butter with the other. Assuming I can reveal the butter, I have to smear it onto the the two crackers without a) snapping the crackers in half (especially if the butter is cold and hard) or b) dropping at least one of the crackers onto the floor of the bus, butter side down of course *why do you even bother wondering*. The chances are high that by now, there's also butter on the lap of my trousers or on the back of the seat in front.

But, all being well, by now I have two crackers caked in butter. Next I have to get rid of the butter wrapper, and fish the cheese out of the bag and liberate it from its tight cladding of thick cellophane, all with one hand and my teeth. There's nowhere to put the crackers down unless the seat next to me is free. But the seat is sloping and furry and has enjoyed the close company of thousands of boys' farting bums over the life of the coach; is that somewhere I really want to rest my food? So I manage the best I can, balancing the buttered crackers on one of my legs and biting the end off the rubbery cheese packet. Hallelujah, I manage to get the cheese out without it flying across the bus. However, the crackers are square, and the cheese is thick and rectangular, like a small brick. The geometry is simply all wrong. Had I a plate, a table and a decent knife, I might just manage to cut the cheese into strips and distribute it across the surface of the crackers. But I have none of these things. Well, there's a plastic knife but it as much good at cutting cheese as a starfish carrying a banjo. No, the only feasible thing to do is to stick the entire chunk of cheese between the two crackers and make a sort of wobbly sandwich. Which is what I do. But no sooner do I take a bite than the whole edifice crumbles and splinters like a paper house in an earthquake, with chunks of my meagre lunch plummeting to the floor and onto my neighbour, assuming I have one, and leaving me wondering if the school's catering manager (whose nickname is Fat Rat) has ever been tasked with eating his dastardly creation.

I give up with the main course and move onto pudding. The Wagon Wheel is easy and easily the most enjoyable part of the meal. Unless I left it by a heating vent, when it is a sticky, marshmallowy mess. I dive back into the bag for the apple and enthusiastically polish it on my chest. But, too late, I discover that I chucked the butter wrapper back into the bag and it left a gob of butter on my Granny Smith, a gob of butter I have just rubbed all over my jacket. And the apple is now covered in a film of grease and fluff.

At fourteen I quit the choir and singing altogether, citing the occasional bullying I suffer for my cherubic voice. The director of music is sacked. It looks as if my music-making days are over.

In a daring move, the headmaster appoints a replacement who is still in teacher-training and singing bass in the Choir of King's College, Cambridge: Ralph Allwood. He is twenty-two, bearded and with a mop of long, wild black hair. He drives an old Ford Anglia with balding tyres. But he's too tied up in Cambridge to be in Pangbourne full-time, so for two terms we have an interim, Philip Doghan, a flamboyant tenor at the beginning of his singing career. We all assume he's gay - on account of the flamboyance and his penchant for high notes - but he isn't. Far from it.

When Ralph Allwood takes up his post, music suddenly becomes cool. The choir becomes something that people want to be in, though I'm not keen to rejoin. What would I sing? I'm unaware of my voice breaking and the last thing I want to do is to be still singing treble with a load of junior squits. So I give the choir a wide berth.

Ralph - he is widely known as Ralph rather than the prescribed Mr Allwood or Sir - recruits a raft of new, young instrumental teachers, mostly old pals from Cambridge. Finally, I get a clarinet teacher, an Oxford undergraduate who opens my eyes to my shortcomings. Richard Cooke, future conductor of the Royal Choral Society, teaches me piano. Stephen Barlow and Roy

Goodman are cajoled into playing the organ for Sunday services. Eventually, Ralph persuades me to have a go at singing and we discover I'm a tenor. I start to have singing lessons and Ralph reckons I could be choral-scholar material. Meanwhile, my father is baulking at the amount of music lessons on the school bill. I'm destined for "something in the City", a chartered accountant probably, like my grandfather; is all this really necessary?

At seventeen I win a choral scholarship to King's College, Cambridge. It turns out I'm Pangbourne's first scholar to Oxbridge in any shape or form, in living memory. The entire school is awarded a half-day holiday in celebration and I've never, ever been more popular. Ralph Allwood, it turns out, is one of the great educators of his generation, if not of several generations.

If Pangbourne hadn't been such an entirely unsuitable school with a deficient head of music, they would never have recruited Ralph and I wouldn't be a singer. I'd probably be working in finance and possibly extremely well-off. I'd drive a Mercedes, and no doubt would have London's City elders nudging me to follow in my father's footsteps up the Corporation ladder...

So that was a stroke of luck.

Eggs Florentine

An interview with Florence Foster Jenkins

CG: Mrs Foster Jenkins... may I call you Florence?

FFJ: No, you may call me Mrs Foster Jenkins.

CG: There's no easy way to ask this...

FF: Yes?

CG: What is it like to be called the worst singer who ever lived?

FFJ: I don't know. You tell me.

CG: Let me put it another way. Are you a very bad singer?

FFJ: Me? I don't think so. Why? Do you think I'm a bad singer?

CG: Well I have heard some some, um, rather alarming recordings.

FFJ: But does that make me a bad singer? I've heard some alarming recordings too, by people who are much more celebrated than I, people who sing in the biggest opera houses in the world. Are you saying they're bad singers too?

CG: Well, no, but...

FFJ: Who has said I'm a bad singer? A critic? You're a singer too aren't you? Do you believe everything critics say or do you hold to the creed, as I most certainly do, that you should believe in yourself and not be deterred by the opinions of critics? In fact, wouldn't you say that the golden rule that nearly every great singer abides by is to not read reviews?

CG: Ah, well, plenty of singers say that, but they do actually read the reviews.

FFJ: Well more fool them then. Why can't they stick to their principles? Where are their guts? Let me tell you, if I listened to every naysayer that dared to damn my work, where would I be today? You don't have to like my singing but you cannot deny that, unlike you, I am a household name. Have you ever sold out the Carnegie Hall?

CG: I've never even sung at the Carnegie Hall…

FFJ: Well there you are then. Need I say more? And anyway, what do you mean "a bad singer"? You mean I fail to express myself through song or that I vocalise badly?

CG: Since you mention it, let's talk about vocal technique.

FFJ: Oh do we have to? I cannot imagine anything more boring for me, for you, or for your readers. How can you possibly be so dull? Name me one truly great singer who has talked interestingly about vocal technique. No, a great singer transcends the limitations of the voice. It's not all breath, support and resonance you know. It isn't even necessarily singing the so-called "right notes" or "right words". Be honest, how many times have you sat in an opera house and been at a loss to understand what's going on? Hmm?

CG: So what is it then?

FFJ: If you have to ask, I cannot possibly explain.

Lentil Soup

1976

"I think there's a composer living next door," my mother says. "I can hear him playing the piano. It sounds pretty horrid if you ask me."

We are still living in the same small house in Knightsbridge and by now the area is fully gentrified. The tiny Italian grocery shop, The Capri Stores, its ceiling once hung with cheeses and salamis, has closed. The butcher and greengrocer on Montpelier Street won't survive for much longer. My mother used to have accounts at all three shops, which my father settled every month. Throughout my childhood, she sent me out to run and fetch groceries. The shopkeepers all knew me, so I would simply ask for whatever was on her list and they would add it to their ledger and put the chops, the onions, the Ribena, the spaghetti in its blue paper wrapper, into my basket for me to carry home.

The Wimpy Bar is now a posh patisserie. The off-licence is now an estate agent. The little mews garage where a potter did her work and where the kids of the neighbourhood like me would hang out all day, has become a chic pied-a-terre. The pub across the road has become a wine bar. Only the house on Montpelier Place which my mother swears is a brothel has stayed the same. As has our house. It still has no central heating. The pre-war gas boiler has finally packed up and the water in the tank is now warmed by an immersion heater. In the winter we rely on electric convection heaters that smell of burning dust. My father has stoppered the old gas pipe in the kitchen with a cork and some duct tape but there's always a slight whiff of gas. The kitchen is in the basement and the lino on the floor regularly bulges off the subfloor in huge blisters as the damp underneath tries to escape. Water arrives at the kitchen sink through dented lead pipes. Woodworms are eating the post-war utility furniture. The overhead fluorescent light hums while the fridge rattles under the stairs that I fell down as a toddler, knocking out a front tooth.

A door leads to what we call the back room but which is actually at the front of the house. It used to be a maid's room in another lifetime but is full of junk. The plaster is falling off the walls in huge mildewed chunks only to lie on the piles of "useful" cardboard boxes that my father hordes but never uses. The freezer lives in this room, covered in patches of rust and dust. My mother rarely bothers to cook properly anymore and the freezer is packed with Findus pies and McCain Oven Chips, buried in a choking permafrost that makes shutting the freezer door near impossible. Deep in the freezer's bowels, like Ötzi the Iceman, who was discovered after thousands of years buried in an Austrian glacier, are legs of lamb and pork chops, inedible and leathered by frozen neglect.

My mother hangs laundry in the back room, on a rack that hangs from a pulley, which adds to the damp. How clothes ever dry is a mystery. At the far end of the room is the old coal store, its iron lid still embedded in the pavement outside. There is still coal in the store, forgotten and redundant since my parents converted the fireplaces to gas. Light just about makes it through grubby glass tiles in the pavement above. Light also comes from the single bulb that hangs from the ceiling on a wire that hasn't been replaced since the 1940s. On the rare occasions my father uses an electric drill in the back room, he plugs it too into the same light fitting. None of the wiring has been updated. My father, in a rare burst of homely zeal, once installed reading lamps above our bunk beds, wiring them to the mains with 12-volt bell wire.

In a small pantry outside the back door live rusty tins of cling peaches and mandarin oranges in syrup, condensed milk and corned beef. Many of the tins are so old that they pre-date the introduction of sell-by dates. And all those that do have sell-by dates are years beyond their expiration.

It may be surprising then that my father is about to become Lord Mayor of London, and that the house will stay in this condition for another twenty-five years. By then the kitchen ceiling, on which my mother regularly bangs with a broom handle to announce that dinner is ready, will have collapsed. It finally happens one night while my father is upstairs on the sofa, eating a Yorkie Bar and watching Coronation Street. There has been a one-inch wide crack in it for some time but my father has declared it "not life-threatening", much like the constant smell of leaking gas, so does nothing about it. My mother has been dead for three years, so the ceiling isn't provoked when it collapses. It just falls down.

My father is not interested in the upkeep of his home. When he has money he spends it on his boat, which he equips to take on fantasy voyages that exist only in his head. The boat, kept mostly in Cowes on the Isle of Wight, has everything a sailor needs to cross an ocean, yet he mostly uses it as a floating caravan with occasional sorties across the Solent or, twice a year, the English Channel. Not that he *should* cross an ocean but the boat - for some reason it is never called a yacht - seems like an indulgence when the family kitchen is falling apart around my mother's ears. During the winter months it is kept in St Katherine's Dock on the Thames and on Sundays they "potter about" on it, which means he smokes his pipe in the wheelhouse while she reads the Sunday papers down below and cooks lunch in the tiny galley kitchen.

Hans Werner Henze is the composer who has moved in next door.

As an eighteen year-old about to head to King's College, Cambridge on a choral scholarship, I've never heard of him. Nor has my mother who's more into Frank Sinatra than German modernism. They're doing his opera *We Come To The River* at Covent Garden. Henze's that is, not Sinatra's.

The house technically belongs to Henze's companion Fausto, though it's Henze who has paid for it and who rules the roost. They only stay there for occasional bouts so it is a while before we meet. A friend of mine at Cambridge asks me if I'll give Henze a message, something banal to do with his festival in Italy, so one morning I press the doorbell. Fausto opens the door and cheerily asks me in.

"Come downstairs to the kitchen. I'll get Hans."

The kitchen is a far cry from ours. Modern, light, clean. Pretty young men are wandering around. Henze appears in his dressing-gown. He has steely eyes, friendly but quite intimidating.

"So you are ze young tenor from next door. I hear you practising." This is unnerving but interesting. How good have I been? I pass on the message from my friend and he invites my family over for drinks later in the week. He is fulfilling a lifetime's ambition to go out to the theatre every night, so it will have to be drinks before he leaves for the West End.

A few nights later my parents and I are in his house again. Fausto opens some very good champagne and we plant ourselves on plush sofas, I next to my mother. The chat is neighbourly, light. Henze turns to me and says: "So perhaps you know my good friend Peter Maxwell Davies?" I know *of* him, but I don't know him, nor can I say I know any of his music. I might have heard something at The Proms but I can't remember. The most modern things I've sung have been pieces knocked up by friends at Cambridge and carols by John Rutter. But I don't want to appear an idiot. I want to impress. And besides, talking serious music is *my* territory. It's *my* thing, not my parents'. They can sit in awe, for a change, while I chat casually about the thing *we* do, *me* and Henze. *Me* and the world-famous composer, as I'm beginning to realise.

I'm just nodding and finding the words to say "Oh, yes, I know Maxwell Davis but not, you know, *personally...*" when my mother, next to me, lubricated with good champagne, chimes in:

"Oooh, yes, he's the one who writes books about otters isn't he?"

My elbow plunges into my mother's side. Henze looks bemused.

"Ha, no, hahaha!" I blurt. "No that's the other chap. Gavin Maxwell, that's him. The otter man. *Ring of Bright Water.*" I redden. Henze blinks.

Henze and Fausto go off to the theatre and a few nights later my parents reciprocate with dinner. It's Sunday - no theatre. Henze is a vegetarian so my mother has to move away from her usual repertoire of meaty staples. We start with lentil soup and Henze declares it amongst the best he has ever eaten. It's just as well he can't see the kitchen in which it was cooked.

I don't see our neighbours much after that. After Cambridge I move into a flat in Fulham with Simon Halsey, the choral conductor, and Thomas Trotter, the organist, both my contemporaries at King's and all three of us ready to kick off our careers. In the mid 80s my agent says that La Fenice in Venice has enquired about my availability to do Henze's *Elegy For Young Lovers* on the recommendation of the composer, which seems remarkably nice of him, considering he has probably only ever heard me through a wall. But I'm not available.

A few years later at Fiumicino airport, I find myself on the same shuttle bus as Henze and Fausto, but I'm feeling shy and they're looking grumpy, so I don't reintroduce myself.

I move onto other flats, then marriage, children... Fairholt Street is still the family home but not where I live. It's only when my first marriage falls apart that I find myself living back there for a few months with my wife-to-be, Lucy Schaufer. My mother and Fausto now get on very well, exchanging keys, swapping gardening tips.

One night, Lucy and I are wandering back from a stroll when Fausto happens to fling open his front door. We stop and say hello. Fausto is quite drunk and as high as a kite. This isn't a surprise. I've smelled pot wafting from their garden. Even my mother has mooted in a whisper that *"they might be pot smokers next door..."*

"Hello, hello!!! Come in for a drink! Come on, come in! Olly is here, Olly Knussen. You must know Olly!"

I've done a couple of things with Olly Knussen; a performance of *Albert Herring* several years before and a Schnittke symphony fairly recently. I haven't really got to know him, yet, but it will be good to say hello.

We sheepishly enter the house, which is still as plush as I remember. Olly and Henze are immersed in soft chairs, clutching big glasses of red wine. They've all been out for dinner. They too are stoned. And giggly. Boy are they giggly. So we drink wine too and try to make small talk but we sense we're really too far behind to be any fun for these three who are gazing into the middle distance and trying desperately to act sober, and after a short while we make our excuses and retreat next door.

A few years later I get to sing not only *Elegy For Young Lovers*, in Amsterdam with Olly conducting, but also Henze's masterpiece *Voices,* several times, in London and

Holland, also with Olly. Henze comes to some of the performances. He's beginning to look frail and a bit wobbly. It could be all the pot he's inhaled over the years, or he could just be off his head during the concerts. But as we take our bows together, I'm still remembering Gavin Maxwell and books about otters.

Suet pudding

There's a type of man in the music business that I keep seeing all over the world. I've never actually seen this man on a plane or bumped into him at an airport, but I'm sure, judging by the look of him, that the only food he eats is airline food. That and first night party food. His teeth are grey and his breath smells of cheap wine and damp theatres.

Over one shoulder he carries an exhausted fake leather bag which is the only luggage he ever uses. In it are a laptop, a large cardboard diary, a pair of underpants which he alternates with the ones he's wearing, and a few kilos of sewing kits and little soaps, gathered from cheap hotels around the world. He's shouldered this bag for so long that he leans to one side, like a fleshy Tower of Pisa.

This, ladies and gentlemen, is a typical opera agent; typical at least of the agents I have tended to have, and I've had lots.

My first I sacked when he got a booking wrong by a whole year. My second is now a dog-breeder and my third has become a school-teacher. My fourth gave it up to be a mother. My fifth became a casting director who has stopped casting me. My sixth was my fourth revisited, making a return after a few years of motherhood, who passed me onto my seventh, who then decided to become a lawyer instead. My eighth also gave it up to be a mother so I moved onto my ninth, an ex-singer whom I've known since conservatoire. He then semi-retired to France while protesting he was still at it full time and that being in a quiet corner of Normandy wouldn't make any difference to his business. It did. So now I'm on my tenth.

With any luck my tenth agent will be my last, if the airline and party food don't finish him off first. When I asked him to represent me I pointed out that he would be managing the twilight of my career, but in the absence of any other old git tenors on his list, he took me on. I'm hoping to get at least seven years out of him until my pension kicks in. Ten, tops.

Agents have a joke: they say their clients are paid 90% of everything the agents earn. I've yet to meet a singer who finds this funny.

Why anyone would want to become an agent is a complete mystery. They have terrible hours: full days in the office and interminable evenings spent traipsing after their clients, lying about how wonderful they were *mwah mwah*. Half of their working day is spent sucking up to awful people - many of whom don't know what they're talking about and who got a job in casting after a move from marketing - the other half handling the fragile egos of their singers, particularly the ones who can't understand why their massive talent is going so unrecognised by the world (while forgetting their own history of cancellations and poor behaviour). They are not well-paid and they live on a diet of Pret-a-Manger sandwiches. They spend hours in airports and in planes, travelling to remote cities to have inconclusive meetings, begging for work for their clients, watching more performances of *La Traviata* than should be allowed under human rights legislation and staying in cheap hotels near the station so that they can catch an early train five hours after going to bed and a full hour before the hotel's dismal buffet breakfast is laid out. They are anglers who spend all day by a shit-filled canal and who have only a rotting shoe to show for a catch. Quite why they want to do it beats me.

--

If you've ever attended the opening night of a new production of *Die Zauberflöte,* you might have thought that by the end of the opera, Tamino's trials were over. You would be wrong, for the tenor still faces his greatest ordeal: The First Night Party.

Yes, a party sounds fun. Lots of free food and wine, a chance to wind down with the colleagues you've been working with for the last four weeks... what's so bad about that? But by the time you've got out of your costume and make-up, put on something smart to wear and joined the party, all you can see is a sea of completely unfamiliar faces. The first night crowd is in - all those agents, intendants and critics - and they've already eaten all the food and drunk most of the drink. Rather than being greeted with smiles, you see people in a much more expensive clothes than yours making slightly disdainful faces in your direction, as if you have come to the party wearing a hat made out of sausages. All your friends from the show are talking to their agents. And because most agents treat singers who aren't their clients like lepers, you avoid them. You are introduced to someone important and try to engage in conversation, but your conversant constantly looks over your shoulder to see who more important than you is in the room. You still don't have any food or drink and you're having to shout at the top of your already exhausted voice because a junior member of the marketing department whose job it was to organise the party thought it would be fun to book a live polka band. By the end of the evening you've swallowed one tiny *hors d'oeuvre* and more bad wine than you really should, given that you've been responsibly avoiding alcohol for the past month...

You get the picture.

Frankly, if I were singing Tamino I'd rather give up halfway through Act 2 and head to a quiet pub with Monostatos and The Queen of The Night. It would be a lot more fun.

Waffles

2015

A hipster is driving down Broadway. The car is old, his face is bearded, he's wearing a plaid shirt and a beanie hat. The window is down and he is yelling. "I AM GOING TO FUCK YOU UP! I AM GOING TO FUCK YOU UP! I AM GOING TO FUCK YOU UP SO BAD AND THEN YOU WILL DIE!"

I have no idea what is his grievance as I stand on the sidewalk and watch him drive by, alone in his car. He is probably on the phone but I can't see one. I'm guessing someone has offered him a coffee from the wrong side of a Colombian valley, and brewed it in a Mr Coffee filter machine. Or they've laughed at him for wearing socks or ironed his drainpipe jeans the wrong way.

This isn't New York's Broadway, it's Chicago's, far north of the city centre in an area called Edgewater. Lake Michigan is just three blocks to the east.

Lucy and I own a small 1920s apartment nearby. Her family is from Chicago. She grew up in its suburbs. So when her parents died, leaving her a modest inheritance, we took the opportunity of depressed house prices to pick up a bargain. Besides, I had recently got a green card, making me a US resident, so we really had to establish that I was serious about that.

There are lots of misconceptions about green cards and I'd fallen prey to most of them. A green card is not simply a work permit. Yes, it allows you to work in the USA, but they expect you to live there too. And if you don't, they seriously want to know why. If you spend too much time out of America they take a dim view. A green card is just shy of being a US citizen, a stepping-stone to citizenship. You don't get to vote, and they can revoke your residency at any time, but otherwise you are expected to behave exactly like an American. You have to fill out a US tax return every year, whether you earn in the USA or not.

Where it becomes really onerous is with all the stuff that until now was none of their business. Any savings, including that ISA you've been building as part of your pension, your house, bank accounts, anything with money in it, they want a part of. You think your ISA is tax-free? Well it may be in the UK but Uncle Sam doesn't care. If your ISA does well, the IRS expects a share, no questions asked. If you move house, in the UK, you will be liable for US capital gains tax.

When I tried to start a new ISA in the UK, the fund company asked me if I was a US resident. Technically I was, so I said yes, and as soon as I did, they refused to do business with me. It's not that it's not allowed, it's that financial institutions would rather do without the hassle of having the IRS breathing down their neck.

My green card did me a fat lot of good. I did one good stretch of work on it at LA Opera but the economy was in disarray, opera houses retreated to the safe ground of Verdi and Puccini and that's not really my bag. Eventually I realised it wasn't worth hanging on to and I gave it up. It's very easy. You just post the card back to the embassy with a form, and that's that.

Of course, the moment I handed back the green card, offers of American work started to come in. And now, every time I fly into the USA, I am grilled by border control.

"Why did you give up your green card?" they ask, as if anyone who does so must be completely dodgy. Who wouldn't want to live in America for heaven's sake. *Are you mad?*

"I'm afraid I was finding that all my work was in Europe and not in America so it really didn't make any sense anymore."

That seems to work. But one border officer replies: "Yeah, I guess you have more culture in Europe. But then again, we don't have all those Muslims." I'm not sure how to react. I know for sure that I'm appalled by such blatant racism in someone wearing a federal uniform, but he has my passport in his hand and I want it in mine so that I can get into the country. I'm so shocked I don't even have the presence of mind to make a note of his name and complain later.

On the strength of a book I wrote called *Who's My Bottom?,* based on my experiences of singing Britten's *A Midsummer Night's Dream,* the baritone Nathan Gunn, head of the post-graduate opera faculty at the University of Illinois, catchily called The Lyric Theatre at Illinois, asks me to direct the opera for his students in early 2016 with rehearsals starting before Christmas. The lack of a green card is not a problem. I'll be on an academic visa, apparently the same whether you're a student or a teacher, and compared to a normal performing visa, they are an absolute piece of piss.

The University of Illinois is not based in Chicago as you might expect, but sandwiched between two towns one-hundred-and-forty miles to the south, Champaign and Urbana, collectively and commonly known as "Chambana". They should really make it official, because it is impossible to know where one town stops and the other begins, and quite honestly, who gives a fuck?

I can't realistically commute from Chicago, but I will be able to go "home" at weekends.

I've never directed before. This could be a laugh. Before I say yes, I spend a few days working out how I want to set it. I've developed a few ideas over the years, but the stumbling block has always been the fairies. Who are they? What are they? How do you come up with a design concept that avoids the usual tropes - wings and pixie ears for starters - yet supports the idea of a group of kids singing as a chorus, led by a king and queen? After a couple of days spent chewing my lip, unable to concentrate on anything else, I have a little eureka moment at four in the morning. Scouts. Or rather, a version of scouts. I email Nathan back and say yes. This is exciting.

I can't pick a design team. These will be post-graduates, assigned by the professors at the Lyric Theatre. My production budget is $18,600 which sounds pretty tiny, but it's for material costs only. There are no labour costs because everything is done in-house by the university. For what I have in mind, $18,600 is more than enough.

Most of the advance work is done online. I have a meeting via Skype with a room full of university faculty heads, my face planted on a fifty inch screen on the wall. I worry that I should have trimmed my nose hairs first. My ideas about how to do the piece don't go down well across the board and one professor wants me to explain at length why I'm not setting it in "the period in which it was written" with tights and togas, which is why I guess he's teaching at a state university and not working on Broadway.

While I'm in Aix-en-Provence singing in a revival of the Robert Carsen production of the *Dream*, I'm Skyping with my set designer José who is at home in Puerto Rico. He's very experienced, far too experienced to still be at university it seems to me, but I'm grateful for that. I've spent months now figuring out how many entrances and exits I need, who has to be seen, who has to be invisible then visible, all the sort of stuff I've never had to worry about before. Just finding somewhere where Tytania and Bottom can sleep for half an act and not be in the way of everyone else is a challenge in itself.

I make my first visit to Chambana in July of 2015. Lucy and I are in the States anyway while she sings for Central City Opera in the Rockies just west of Denver, followed by a family get-together in Payson, Arizona. All we have to do, in my British mind, is pop in to the University of Illinois on the drive from Arizona to Chicago.

"DRIVE?" says my wife. She may be short but she can be loud. "ARE YOU NUTS?" (I thought we had settled that by now). "It's about two thousand miles!"

"More like one thousand seven hundred actually. I looked it up. We can do Route 66, stay in some fun motels."

My idea of a fun motel is diametrically opposite to my dear wife's. On our honeymoon we stayed in The Wagon Wheel Motel in San Luis Obispo in California during a road trip up the west coast. We ate dinner in the motel bar, where a beardy Steely Dan tribute band played old-fashioned rock in a corner for beer and tips. Our waitress was Tracee, the second syllable much higher in pitch than the first, an over enthusiastic blond with a rictus smile who never blinked and whose blouse was unzipped down to between her breasts. We had the Chicken 'n' Rib Combo, a plate of brown deep-fried glory that was still ice-cold in the centre. We didn't complain for fear of it coming back with an extra seasoning of the chef's phlegm. At three in the morning, we were awoken by loud music thumping from a car outside our room, its engine still running. I went to the window to tell them to turn the radio down, in my best public school accent, but before I could get there Lucy hissed "GET AWAY FROM THE WINDOW! DRUG DEAL!" Personally I loved the whole experience. But then again, I love diners and distrust most "fancy" restaurants in America because they're usually pretentious and have silly things on the menu like "steak served with *au jus*", and the food nearly always arrives too fast to be trustworthy. While Lucy checked airfares between Arizona and Chicago - she was buggered if we were going to drive - I researched motels on Route 66. When I discovered we could stay in the Boots Court Motel in Carthage, Missouri, a motel so old and venerated it used to be called just The Boots Court because the term "motel" hadn't been coined yet, I won the argument. Not only that, we could stop in Pie Town, New Mexico on the way there, a town which is, yes, famous for its pies. Even though it would add an hour to our journey, I mean, come on, how can anybody *not* stop at a town called Pie Town?

I like motels because they don't pretend to be anything but a convenient place to stop and sleep. You don't expect service, just a room with all the stuff you need when you're asleep, like darkness and a bed. And if you want to leave in the middle of the night, you just go.

Nothing, but nothing, will induce me to stay in an American B&B any more. We've only stayed in a couple but they were both run by people I could politely describe as needy fucking psychopaths. The first, in Springfield, the Illinois state capital, was run by a small, very camp man called Brian. Brian collected stuff. Lots of stuff. And he kept the stuff in the bedrooms that he rented out in his large Victorian house.

Our room had piles and piles of old bakelite radios, all piled up on top of each other. In piles. We were supposed to find them interesting, cute even. But there was nowhere to put anything down, every flat surface being filled with dusty radios, none of which worked. A large family was staying in the next room and in the middle of the night the grandfather suddenly started yelling at the top of his voice. One of his teenage grandchildren chimed in with "oh pleeeeeease shut the fuck up!", then a parent: "don't speak to your grandpa that way!" Grandpa continued to yell, but no-one did anything, as if this were a regular occurrence, Vietnam flashbacks perhaps, and nothing ever worked to calm him down. After about fifteen minutes he fell quiet again.

Despite having paid more than the cost of a normal hotel, for the sheer thrill I presume of staying in a creaky old house called Ye Olde Bed and Breakfast (it wasn't, but it could have been), there was a narrow window of time for breakfast. So we descended for our "Breakfaste Fayre", tired and bemused by the night-time kerfuffle, at eight-thirty. The family from the next room was already sat down, the teenagers sulky, the adults - grandpa especially - completely oblivious to any disturbance they had caused.

The cooked breakfast was strange, curiously sticky-sweet. The owner, Brian, expected us to fawn and smother him with compliments. "Do you love my potatoes? Aren't they delicious? It's my secret recipe. What I do is I cook them in apple juice which makes them so sweet and yummy." Well, so much for that secret. It being America, there was sugar in the bacon and sausage too. There always is though God knows why. So the only unsweetened thing on the plate was the pile of scrappy, overcooked scrambled eggs, though I wouldn't have put it past Brian to slather those in maple syrup and pop a marshmallow on top for good measure.

Our second B&B experience was in Lancaster County, Pennsylvania. This is Amish country and a hotbed of tourism. It has towns called Intercourse and Paradise, so what's not to like?

112

From the outside, the B&B looked like a fine old stone house, with some out-of-place sculpture-porn planted in front; a life-size bronze of a naked woman with impossibly perky tits. She looked like she was posing for Playboy. Clearly this place wasn't run by the Amish.

The owner, all big hair and faux-gentility, greeted us. But before she would show us to our room we had to have a tour of the house, starting in the lounge, which was lavishly decorated in a style I like to call Post-Colonial Shit. "The needlework is all by me." It was everywhere, on chairs, tables, the curtains. On the walls were framed examples of her work, dusky maidens with an exposed breast or bare bum. There were puppies, kittens and horses, all expertly stitched but all truly terrible.

I spotted a needlework view of Amsterdam. "Ah, Amsterdam!" I said, desperately trying to find something positive to say out loud. She looked quizzical, annoyed even, as if *she* was supposed to point that out, not I. Besides, we still hadn't lathered her with gushing compliments on her artistry. *What's wrong with these people?*

"Yes, my husband is Dutch. He makes our FAMOUS DUTCH PANCAKES for breakfast." She looked expectant, waiting for us to say "Oh my oh my! I don't expect we'll get a wink of sleep as we'll be so excited to try those!" But we didn't. And that too was *bad*. Clearly, we were going to be difficult guests, something which pleased me enormously. The woman was clearly a snob and now I just needed to find ways to irk her.

She showed us the visitors book, indicating where we should say something nice when we leave. It was full of syrupy platitudes and I was already wondering how to write "your needlework is absolute crap" without her coming after us swinging a cast-iron pancake pan. "Yes, right, we'll get around to that later" we said.

She took us to our room which had also been furnished at great expense but with excruciating taste; all gold taps and frilly drapes. It had a four-poster bed (don't they all?), and again we failed to swoon adequately. She handed us a laminated card of HOUSE RULES, turned on her heel and left us to unpack.

And for this bollocks we were paying three times the price of a Motel 6.

In the morning we dutifully ate the FAMOUS DUTCH PANCAKES and they were nothing special, a bit floury and stodgy. I would have much preferred American pancakes. They weren't helped on their way down by some elderly Tea Party types on the next table who were mouthing off about Barack Obama, moaning that America was "going to hell in a handbasket with that SOB in the White House". Clearly they felt that this B&B was a fine, conservative establishment, where regurgitating Fox News drivel at the top your voices was perfectly acceptable, the only pity being that there was evidently a couple of LIBTARDS at the next table pushing their pancakes around their plates, failing to be polite and conversational, him with his suspicious English accent and all.

Before we checked out and made a point of *not* signing the visitors book - that showed 'em - we caught a brief glimpse of the FAMOUS DUTCH HUSBAND who looked like he had just stepped out of the Dutch comedy, *Flodder*, wearing sharply-creased, shiny trousers and shiny grey shoes, his hair a slicked-back mullet. I'd bet all the money in my wallet that he had a red leather blouson jacket in his wardrobe. And a medallion.

--

Come the summer, we drive from Payson, Arizona to Tucumcari, New Mexico on the first day, stopping for an excellent slice of cherry pie in Pie Town. I chew over the possibility that there could be many other remote towns named after excellent experiences; Blowjobsville, Fartworth, Handshandy City, Haircut... these are just a few that spring to mind.

A lot of the journey is spent driving alongside the Sante Fe Railroad, in the company of surprisingly frequent goods trains, most of them a mile long, being hauled by two engines. In Tucumcari, we stay in the Motel Safari, right on the old Route 66, and eat at a greasy spoon up the road. Bar a few more motels and gas stations, that is the whole of Tucumcari, a two mile strip that most people drive by on Interstate 40, bypassing the old "mother road". [3]

The next day we push on through Texas and Oklahoma, into the bottom left hand corner of Missouri and the Boots Court Motel, Carthage.

The motel is tiny and built differently to a conventional post-war motel. It is basically a row of parallel cabins with

---

[3] Movie buffs might be interested to hear that Tucumcari features in the Coen brothers' *The Ballad of Buster Scruggs* as the remote and desolate location of the bank in the chapter *Near Algodones.*

a single roof spanning the whole group of huts. You park your car under the roof, between two cabins and step straight into your room. The motel had stared demolition in the face - nobody really stops in Carthage any more - but was rescued by two middle-aged sisters who are restoring it, bit by bit. I thought the place would be tough to get into, given it's almost a national monument, and I phoned months in advance to secure a room. But when we get there it seems we are only one of two couples booked in for the night. One of the sisters checks us in.

"So, how much do you know about the Boots Motel?" she asks, hearing my accent and clearly hoping I'll say "absolutely nothing", which would be odd, given I'd booked so far in advance and surely a clue I've done some research. "Oh I've read all about it on your website" isn't the correct response, even though I hope it might forestall the history lecture I can see coming over the horizon, but it's what I say nonetheless.

Undeterred - this is possibly her only social interaction for the day - she gives us the full history, which is just what we want after seven hours of driving. We dutifully oooh and aaah, and interject the odd "really? That's fascinating" if we think it might move the process along. I spend as much of the history lecture as I can at the other end of the tiny reception, pretending to examine postcards and pamphlets, where I let out a succession of post-long-drive farts as silently and odourlessly as I can.

We are given the Clark Gable room, so-called because during WWll, Gable had an army friend who lived nearby and he would stay in the motel, in *this very room.* The bed is small by motel standards, just a conventional double, topped with a candlewick bedspread. They have installed a retro-style radio tuned to a 1940s music station and there is no TV. It's adorable and exactly the sort of room that any traveller who isn't interested in actual history rather than the phoney B&B stuff would bitch and moan about. "Where's the mini-bar? The WiFi sucks! No TV? This is bullshit!"

Sadly, Carthage is a dreary town but looks like it was once fine and prosperous, with an imposing town square bordered by grand shops, now mostly vacant, and an impressive old stone courthouse in its centre. This is small town America today. I've seen it all over the country and it's deeply depressing. For breakfast the next day we visit a newly set-up coffee shop in the square which is mostly empty save for the occasional lawyer popping in for a takeaway coffee before he heads to the courthouse. My guess is it will be out of business by the end of the year. The few shops there are - shambolic "antique emporiums" and vendors of mobility equipment for the elderly - have no customers. Anyone who is shopping at this time of day is at WalMart or having a coffee in Dunkin' Donuts at a strip mall on the outside of town.

We arrive at the University of Illinois the next day and I launch into two days of design meetings while Lucy drives on to Chicago alone. I've never really participated in meetings before, certainly not with so many people. Universities love meetings. Any opportunity, someone calls a meeting. It doesn't take me long to figure out that the best thing to do at a big meeting is to let everyone else talk while you doodle meaningfully in a notebook. If you say something, somebody else will want clarification on what you said and then suggest another, smaller meeting involving someone else who isn't at this meeting so that you can go over the points raised, clarify them in an inter-departmental email for consideration at the next extra-departmental meeting. Then you all have to get your diaries out to find a time to meet to arrange the meeting after that... and so on and so on. But compared to singing, it's a doddle.

The designers are a lovely bunch and have come up with some early sketches. José has even built a small maquette of the set and it's all rather exciting. In three months we'll start rehearsing.

I am given a tour of the Krannert Center, which is where we'll do my show. *My show*, ha! It's extremely impressive, a vast arts centre with a two thousand-seat symphonic hall and three theatres. We'll be in the Tryon Festival Theatre, the largest, which seats about one thousand. I march up and down the auditorium checking to see how the sightlines will be, asking questions about rigging and lighting, hoping it makes it look like I have some clue how to direct. I reckon if you've hired someone to direct merely on the basis of their ability to write a funny book, you might want some reassurance. I think I made it clear to them I've never actually directed before. I hope so.

At the end of November, I drive again to Champaign-Urbana, this time from Dallas where Lucy is working. About midway between the two is a motel, in a small town called Bald Knob, Arkansas, so of course that's where I break my journey for the night. Bald Knob? Who wouldn't? The motel is full of hunters. Their pick-up trucks are adorned with a combination of NRA stickers, biblical quotes and comedy testicles dangling from the tow hook. As I check in, one of the hunters is pulling some six-packs of beer from the back of his truck which he takes to a nearby room. It sounds like a blokey party is in full swing.

In the morning, I get up well before dawn, even before the hunters, and continue driving north-east. I cross the White River wetlands as the sun is rising. The light is strange and magical. I keep telling myself I should stop to photograph one of the farmhouses that I pass on the way. They look extraordinary draped in the pink-blue mist. But I have a long drive ahead of me and I can't keep stopping for photo-ops or I'll never make it. Besides, I worry that a farmer will spot me and take exception at some poncy Brit photographing his property without his say-so. This is Arkansas after all. They shoot to kill.

While I'm driving, stopping only for coffees, petrol or waffles at the Waffle Inn, Blytheville - a town which may have induced feelings of blitheness once but which is now a grim strip of shitinesss; time for a renaming ceremony I think - I am turning over in my head what I'll say at my introduction when we start rehearsals tomorrow. Very little, I decide.

119

I've said it before, there are several things I've never understood about the way that opera is put on. Chief amongst these is the secrecy that surrounds "the concept". This has been agreed a long time ago. The designs are all in place, the set is being the built, the costumes too. So why keep the cast in the dark, the people who actually have to perform the piece, until the first day of rehearsals? It's bonkers. Far better surely to have them know the world in which they'll be playing before they learn their roles rather than afterwards? Otherwise they may think they'll be in togas and tights rather than what the director has in mind. Yet, throughout my singing career, not once have I been told what to expect. It's always "OK, THIS is how we are going to do it, in a lunatic asylum where everyone is stark naked! Now *three, four, and off you go...*"

So, I write a backstory for the production and I have it emailed to everyone involved, months before we kick off with rehearsals. Faced with the limitations of doing *A Midsummer Night's Dream* with a young and inexperienced cast, my hunch is that I should pick a concept where it makes sense that everyone is roughly the same age but also one which they cast will understand because, hopefully, it relates strongly to their own experiences. So, no, no togas, tights or anything "traditionally" Shakespearian as I don't see that meaning anything personal to a soprano from Saratoga or a tenor from Tulsa. And besides it doesn't offer me much opportunity to find new laughs in the opera. As far as I'm concerned, a *Dream* production which isn't funny (as well as a bit mad) is doing it wrong. The fairies pose a particular challenge because most people, when they hear the word "fairy" think of prissy little creatures with wings who do only good. This is a Victorian conceit, pushed to its limits by Walt Disney, and has nothing to do with Shakespeare.

I send this to the cast:

> Athens is a small, white-picket-fence town in New Hampshire, population 11,351, where the Duke family has dominated for nearly 200 years. Theseus Duke Snr owns a local mill, several farms in the area, an equestrian centre, a maple syrup business, the town's department store and a Greek-themed restaurant called The Minotaur. He's served as Mayor for 18 years. A large oak tree in the woods outside of town was planted by his great-grandfather and it is known as The Duke's Oak. Amongst the many other memorials and endowments that Theseus Duke Snr has set up, Athens High School (whose football team are known as *The Athenian Donkeys*) awards a student drama prize once a year. The final of the competition is held at the Senior Prom and awarded by the Prom King (which this year happens to be Duke's son, Theseus Jnr (known in school as The Duke, Dukester, El Dukerino...)), without doubt the most popular and respected young man in the school. Seniors from the school form ad-hoc groups to compete for the prestigious drama award, which is paid out in the form of a

modest annual scholarship. One team this year has called itself The Rustics.

Athens's local wood is occupied by fairies. No-one, least of all the fairies themselves, know where they came from. Entirely human in physical appearance, apart from their extremely pale, moon-ish skin and bright red hair, they could, to all intents and purposes, be from outer space. They've lived in the woods for many centuries and the only humans with whom they have any interactions are from a local tribe, almost extinct, of Native Americans. Indeed, one of the tribe's baby boys has been left in the care of Tytania, the fairy queen. In spite of their immortality, in many ways the fairies aspire to be human, dressing like humans too. Living in the woods, the people they most commonly see are Scouts on camping trips, and so it was in the 1940s that Oberon and Tytania decided that all fairies would henceforth wear their own version of a Scout outfit. (Apart from being an appealing and suitable uniform, this was also far more practical than the pilgrim outfits that they'd worn for the previous 400 years. No humans seemed to wear those any more.)

The period is around 1980/90, contemporary even (without cellphones), but whereas The Rustics seem to be from the present, Theseus Duke and his preppy, high school friends, The Lovers, seem to hark back to a more romantic era, the mid 1950s. Above all, it's a dream. We "have but slumbered here while these visions did appear." Time is immaterial; there are no anachronisms in a dream.

Girl Scout Cookies

2015

At the director's introduction I say something about how, in my experience, director's introductions are usually very dull and confusing. All I ever want to know is what my costume will look like and what the set looks like. I say we will talk about individual character, individually, but I don't want to waste time talking about it without rehearsing it; as soon as the designers have shown their designs, we'll start work.

I talk for about a minute, tops.

I hand over to my team, José Diaz (set), Aimee Beach (costumes) and Danni Deutschmann (lighting). José and Aimee have had about six months of me saying "I want this...we need *this*...hmmm, no, I don't want *that!*" simply because I have been developing very specific ideas about how this will all work, and particularly about what jokes I want to crack, visually and dramatically. I know almost nothing about lighting so Danni will have to put up with me accepting or rejecting her suggestions once we are on stage, though I do want certain effects at certain times but I don't know how to achieve them. The best I can do is say "when magic juice gets squirted in anybody's eyes I want the moon to go all wobbly and the lights to go woooobluhbluhbluhplunk." That seems pretty clear to me.

José's set looks like a decaying school hall that has been swallowed by a forest. It's basically the same set throughout bar some trees that fly in and out to change the density of the forest. Tytania's "nest" is on top of a cave set upstage and out of the way. There are lots of ways to enter and leave the stage, which makes my life a lot easier.

The Lovers will be dressed like rich blue-bloods. The clothes suggest the 1950s but they could be worn by wealthy kids today[4]. Lysander and Demetrius wear khakis and letterman sweaters, each bearing a large A for Athens. These are the "weeds of Athens" that confuse Puck. Hermia and Helena are in mid-length summer dresses. When Lysander meets Hermia for their elopement, she has brought two suitcases. The only luggage he brings is his bag of golf-clubs.

The Rustics are nerds, except for Bottom who's a jock, a football-player. He's involved because Quince is his cousin on his mum's side. They get talking about it at a family barbecue and, to Quince's surprise, Bottom volunteers to be involved. The nerds dress like nerds, so that's easy (and cheap). Starveling, who plays the Moon, habitually wears a NASA t-shirt. Bottom wears a letterman jacket. On the front is a big A, but on the back is an image of the football team's mascot, a donkey.

---

[4] On a local radio show I have to defend my choice of a mixing 1950s clothing with contemporary dress. I point out that in Britain, a prince will regularly climb out of a brand new car, wearing a suit that could have been worn in the 1930s, his wife in the latest fashion, the car doors held open by footmen in 18th century costume, and no-one bats an eyelid. You only have to look at any theatre audience to realise that we don't all dress to one generation's aesthetic.

Tytania and Oberon are in glammed-up scout leader outfits. He has a fur collar and she a large cape. Puck is an overachiever, his scout costume covered in badges. When Oberon loses his temper with him in Act 2, he tears badges off his uniform. The four solo fairies are being sung by female undergraduates and the chorus by a local choir who turn out to be all-girl too. They might not be what Britten had in mind, but they're very good and it serves to sharpen up the idea that Oberon and Puck are the lone males in an all-female society. Nearly all the scout costumes are bought on Ebay at a pittance.

The transformation into the "Prom" scene is very simple. A disco ball and some bunting descend from the flies and the trees are filled with fairy lights. The upper classes are in evening dress.

For the play scene, most of the costumes are bought online. My thinking is that, since the Rustics are nerds, they are giving the play a nerdy theme, so Pyramus and Thisbe are played as Luke Skywalker and Princess Leia from *Star Wars*. Aimee, the costume designer, wonders whether it should be Han Solo but I insist it has to be Skywalker if only to underline the idea that Pyramus and Thisbe's love is forbidden because they are actually brother and sister, a detail I don't expect anyone to pick up unless they stumble upon it while thinking about the show in the bath. It's a slow-burn sort of joke. But I like the idea of Quince, like me, fretting over a design concept and landing on the same solution. They commit suicide using a plastic light sabre. How could you do it any other way?

We choose particularly cheap *Star Wars* costumes. The tackier the better, we reckon. Starveling swaps his NASA t-shirt for a sweatshirt Aimee has found of a wolf howling at the moon. His thornbush is a small, fake Christmas tree and he has a robot toy dog. Snug wears a lion onesie, again bought on Ebay. Apparently normal people sit at home and wear these. Snout too wears a onesie which has been painted with a brick pattern.

Bottom's ass costume is a poser, as it always is. We decide to keep it simple, nothing more than a tail and a head made as an open, ass-head shaped frame, made from basket willow.

--

If I have another bugbear with the way opera is usually done, that bugbear is the rehearsal schedule. Too often, and this may sound incredible, directors have a very sketchy idea of who is in which scene. This is particularly true of directors who have never been performers. With this vague idea of who is on where, they delegate the responsibility of making the rehearsal schedule to an assistant who, more often than not, has an even sketchier idea of who is on where and only the vaguest idea of how long it will take the director to set each scene. All an assistant director is usually interested in is furthering their own career by burying their nose up the director's arse, so the chances are that the assistant will be wildly over-cautious with their schedules. The result is that singers get called to rehearsals for scenes they're not in and the director finds they have been scheduled just half-an-hour to stage a scene that apparently needs two hours. Then a bunch of singers arrive after half-an-hour to rehearse the next scene and are left hanging around for one-and-a-half hours. This leads to grumpiness all round. Believe me. The worst scenario for the assistant director is when they assume a scene will take two hours to stage but it's done in half the time, leaving the director stalled and impatient to move on to another scene.

Given half a chance, assistant directors will call *all* the singers *all* the time just so that their boss will never turn to them and say "WHERE'S SO-AND-SO? WHY AREN'T THEY HERE?"

All this means that, as a singer, you can find yourself being summoned to a foreign city to work, only to be not called for rehearsal, at all, for a whole week, simply because no-one bothered to work out whether you'll actually be needed or not. Even though my cast is stuck in Chambana being students, I'd rather not waste their time and cope with the resentment this can cause.

I reckon this can all be avoided if I spend some time doing my homework. I'm certainly not going to leave it to someone else, given that no-one else on the project has a fraction of my knowledge of this particular opera. I'm supposed to be the expert. That's why they hired me. Handing it off to someone else would be like Andy Murray asking a ball boy to figure out how to beat Roger Federer. Do-able but not the best wisest course of action for getting the job done.

I make a meticulous character plot, specifying who exactly is in each scene. I even specify who is in a scene but inactive (e.g. asleep) so that an over-enthusiastic stage manager doesn't call someone to a rehearsal so simply to lie on the ground for three hours. The character plot means I can also guide my choreographer-cum-assistant Catherine Hamilton through the opera to understand when she can take groups off to another studio for dance calls while I work with another group in the main studio.

And as for scheduling... I spend *hours,* whole days sometimes, working on the rehearsal schedule, and it is time well-spent. It certainly gives me a clear idea of the pace at which I'll have to work to get it all done, especially as many of the roles are double-cast and I'll have to rehearse some scenes twice.

I'm a martyr to a good schedule, me.

--

Many of the singers aren't as well-prepared as I would like. They're all clutching their scores, even when I'm staging physically complex scenes. It looks like they have been trained to work this way. Every time I tell them some moves, they all write them in their scores. That's all very well but it doesn't allow me room to change my mind or for them to suggest something else. They're young though. They don't have the confidence to say "instead of that, how about I try this?" Old fart that I am, when I'm singing I very rarely write any moves in my score anymore. This is partly because I rarely bring a score to rehearsals - I've memorised the thing so it seems redundant - and partly because directors so often change their mind that submitting stage moves to paper often feels like a waste of time.

Even with their scores in front of them, many of the singers are getting the music all wrong, which is worrying to say the least. I find myself slipping into singer-musician mode and cueing them back into the right place, which isn't my job at all on this gig. It means I'm looking down at my score trying to help them out, when I need to be looking at the stage. I have to insist on more coachings for everyone or we'll never the get the show open.

At the end of an early rehearsal one of my Tytanias says something that gives me an idea. She *loves* the scout concept and wonders if we can work in her eating Girl Scout Cookies as she loves those too...

Brits should draw up a comfy chair while I explain about Girl Scout Cookies.

Every year the Girl Scouts of America sell boxes of cookies to raise money for the movement. There's usually a big drive in February (when our show will be performed) and every middle class home will buy several boxes. They used to be home-baked but are now manufactured. They come in several different flavours, but there's no doubt that Thin Mints, crunchy mint in a chocolate shell, are the most popular and, I dare say, iconic. They tend to be kept in, and eaten straight from, the freezer. Any American can recognise a box of Girl Scout Thin Mints from one hundred yards or so, I reckon. Certainly from the back of a theatre.

This gives me the opportunity for several more gags. I've been chewing for a long time how to do the scene where Peaseblossom, Moth, Mustardseed and Cobweb entertain Bottom in the middle of Act 2. It is normally my least favourite scene. Britten can't quite help himself and it all becomes a bit cute, especially when the fairies get out their instruments and play for Bottom and Tytania. Why do they suddenly have instruments on them? I reckon Girl Scout Cookies can come to the rescue and rid us of some of the cute. Or rather, make more sense of the cute.

Tytania summons the four fairies, and when they arrive they have come straight from the kitchen. They are wearing chef hats and aprons, and in their hands pots, pans, spoons and whisks. Our props mistress does a great job coating the insides of the pans with mint-coloured goo. The fairies get to play pissed-off because Tytania has interrupted them in the midst of making Girl Scout Cookies. Yes, okay it's cute. But it's not *cutesy*.

When Bottom sings "Let's have the tongs and the bones", instead of the woodblocks, baby cymbals and recorders that Britten specifies, we take a liberty. This liberty is partly propelled by the fact that none of the fairies has any idea how to play a recorder and no-one on the music staff has realised that this is quite crucial. We use kazoos instead and rather than a woodblock (because fairies *always* carry woodblocks...), Moth uses two inverted saucepans which she hits with wooden spoon, and Mustardseed claps saucepan lids together instead of cymbals. I'm not sure Britten would approve, but I think it's a great improvement.

131

I put in a request that we can have real girl scouts selling cookies in the foyer during the interval. Everyone thinks is an excellent idea, and another way to get some punters in. But the university says we cannot. Something to do with not being seen to be promoting a belief system on university property or something daft. Calls are made to the president of the university and special dispensation is granted. Stalls are set up and loads of cookies are sold. I really don't care too much about that; I just want the audience to be very aware of Girl Scout Cookies, Thin Mints in particular.

After the interval the audience returns to the auditorium for Act 3. When Bottom wakes up he sings his dream monologue. During the passage "The eye of man hath not heard, the ear of man hath not seen, man's hand is not able to taste, his tongue to conceive nor his heart to report what my dream was", while Bottom is trying to figure out what has happened, I have him discover something in the pocket of his letterman jacket: a box of Girl Scout Thin Mints, a memento of his night in the fairy world On the first night, when this moment comes I am biting my nails, worrying that the audience won't get it. When they get it, I allow myself a little "yessss!" from my seat in the stalls.

These are the things I learn about being a director:

- As a director I tell myself I mustn't demonstrate, show them how to play it. With the singers playing roles I've done, I generally manage to avoid this. I don't want them imitating me, I want them finding

132

their own performance. With the other roles, I find myself less disciplined and my excuse is that I'm in the same process of discovery. *If I were doing this for the first time, how would I play this scene?* Sometimes singers want some demonstration, especially when they're inexperienced, but it's best to avoid it if you can.

- Acting out opera scenes in your hotel room is tricky when the furniture is in the way.

- With some singers the best plan is to do everything in your power to stop them ACTING. Our Snug is a case in point. It takes a while but eventually the penny drops that he's much funnier when he's doing nothing. It helps him get the notes right too.

- In rehearsal you lose all sense of time. It's just as well my trusty stage manager Nick is at my side to brew coffee and to tell me how much time we have left before breaks. Without him, I would just keep ploughing on. As often as not he brews a whole pot of coffee at the start of the rehearsal and I'm so busy working I have no time to drink even half a cup.

- I never notice when anyone is a bit late for the start of rehearsal. Chances are I've been there for half an hour already and there's always something to do. Everything becomes a bit blurred. This makes me feel much better about the times I too, as a singer, have been late. Still, I don't condone it as a habit. Naughty Chris. Don't do it again.

- It's a funny thing but I don't take much notice about the quality of anyone's voice. If someone sings all the time, or if they mark, I don't care just as long as they a) do it in the right place and b) give me the right intention and with conviction. All those years I've wondered if a director likes the way I sing something? Complete waste of time. What you don't want to see is someone who's nervous, disruptive or indifferent.

- When a scene works it is the best feeling in the world. On the other hand, after watching something you've staged over and over again, you can get quite bored with what you've done. It seems to me you have to trust it and not keep fiddling with it just to keep yourself interested.

- Taking notes in a dark theatre is very difficult. Getting someone else to take them for you is a skill I've yet to acquire.

- Watching a first night of your production is like being a child again, watching other kids play with *your* toys. First and foremost you don't want them breaking *your* rules and smashing up *your* toys.

- You can have a lot of fun taking the piss out of your conductor by constantly calling him MAESTRO in a deeply sarcastic voice, and because you're the director there's sod-all he can do about it.

Meat balls

A quiz for opera students, much in the style of an American university exam, to find out how they go about preparing a 20th century score:

1) You are offered a role. Do you:

a) Spend the next three months posting on Facebook about how excited you are to be singing the role, "liking" the comments from all your friends who are squealing about how excited they are for you while privately hating your guts?

b) Diligently mark up the vocal score?

c) Go to the gym?

2) The score is fairly difficult. Tonal, but with slightly complex rhythms. Do you:

a) Spend weeks at the piano, figuring out the pitches and rhythms?

b) Listen to a CD a few times in the hope that it sinks in by osmosis?

c) Post a picture of yourself on Facebook, fresh from the gym?

3) The role isn't long but there are many ensembles. Do you:

a) Keep singing the aria you have, over and over again, because that's the only bit that's important, right?

b) Catch the latest Marvel movie?

c) Spend hours at the piano, figuring out the pitches and rhythms?

4) Rehearsals are due to start in a few days. Do you:

a) Take the opera to a coach, to make sure you have it all memorised?

b) Take the opera to a coach in the hope he can teach you the notes?

c) Take the opera to a coach and ask him how long he spends in the gym?

5) Rehearsals begin. Do you:

a) Hope like hell that you get to do the aria soon?

b) Make up any pitch, rhythm, words you like because, hey, it's modern music and who's going to know? It's not like it's Verdi or anything...

c) Make a few mistakes, but with the help of the conductor and repetiteur, correct them without holding up the entire progress of the rehearsal?

Grilled Trout

Cologne, Germany, January 1st 2000

I ring my father to wish him a happy new year, a happy new millennium even. My mother has been dead for three years and I'm aware he has few close friends. In fact I'm not sure he has any. Certainly there's no-one in whom he confides or to whom he can turn for help or advice. There are plenty of people who call him a friend but I can think of nobody who actually treats him as a friend, who would call him up for a chat, or who would ask him out for a drink or a meal.

I doubt he has seen in the new millennium with anyone but the telly. That's the telly which is in exactly the same place in the sitting room that looks exactly the same as it was when I was a child, in the house that's also entirely exactly the same as it was when I was a child. The kitchen ceiling has been replaced, after it collapsed while he watched Coronation Street and ate a Yorkie Bar upstairs, but the rotting kitchen units are the same and the gas tap is still sealed with a cork and duct tape.

The rest of Knightsbridge is not the same as when I was a child. Not even Harrods, which used to be quaint but elegant. It is now gaudy and tacky. It has even lost its catchphrase that, as a boy, I never understood, but which I eventually realised was the very model of English passive-aggression: *The parcel you take home arrives without delay!* The pub across the street that became a wine bar has closed for good. The dry-cleaner at the end of the street has been converted into a fancy residence. There are no grocery stores nearby, but the area is well-served by high-end estate agents, art galleries and yacht brokers. The neighbouring houses are owned by corporations or holding companies and are rarely occupied. If it doesn't fall down out of neglect, our tiny, two-bedroom family home could be worth a ridiculous amount of money.

There is a good reason for my father's lack of friends. Since being Lord Mayor of London twenty-four years ago, he has become so boring he could dig a channel tunnel. The root of his tediousness is his pomposity and the root of his pomposity is his narcissism.

Being a Lord Mayor is dangerous for anyone who responds well to flattery because, for a whole year, that's all that all you get. Now, many Lord Mayors (my grandfather included, because he was one too, in 1958) are capable of understanding that most people in the City of London couldn't give a crap who's Lord Mayor. He's just the king for the year, yet another powerless, balding white man who rides around in a gold coach for a morning, throws a few banquets and cuts lots of ribbons. I bet if I asked anyone in the City to name the current Lord Mayor they would be completely stumped. Heck, I'm a liveryman, a freeman of the City no less, and I haven't a clue.

Yet, for a whole year, he lives in a mansion and is regularly addressed as "My Lord Mayor". People bow to him. They fawn, they suck up. But they're fawning on the office, not the man.

Being Lord Mayor costs a bomb. The Lord Mayor pays for staff at the Mansion House and he foots the bill, personally, for a couple of huge banquets. Had my grandfather not covered the cost, my father would not have been able to afford it. Any semblance of democracy in the election of the Lord Mayor is phoney; it's a post that can only be filled by the wealthy and people who know the right people. No-one criticises the Lord Mayor, they just tell him how marvellous he is. It requires no real acumen beyond not falling over and doing a bit of waving. He doesn't even have to work at weekends. It's Donald Trump's dream job.

As Lord Mayors go, my father is probably pretty good at it, but as far as I know, no-one keeps a tally. A Lord Mayor does his or her job (two women have got the gig in nine hundred-odd years) and at the end of the year it's the next-in-line's turn.

After his stint is over my father seems to harbour a fantasy that he will be recalled at any moment, like a retired diva sitting in the stalls at Covent Garden hoping the second-rate Tosca she is witnessing will crash and burn so that she can leap on stage and save the show.

My father is good at making speeches, there's no doubt about that. Given an audience, he can rabbit on for fifteen minutes without any prepared text or notes. After his mayoral year is over, he is asked by an agency if he would be interested in doing some stints as a professional speaker. He is quoted sizeable fees, but such is his fondness for the sound of his own voice that he is happy to offer his services for absolutely nothing. The agency, dumbfounded, insists that he really should accept fees;

many others do. No, he would rather have the chance to show-off than take anyone's money. This is not good news for an agent wanting his ten percent, so it's no surprise my father gets no more offers for cushy speaking engagements at a thousand quid for ten minutes.

Phone calls with my father follow a pattern. He usually doesn't ask about what's going in my life, let alone what's up with his grandchildren. We really don't converse at all. He just reels off a list of the banquets he's been to in the last week, the committee meetings, the cuttings of ribbons, the occasional brief encounters with minor members of the royal family, while I wonder how long it will be before I can get him off the line. He can't get enough of the royals. I once stood between him and the phone in his kitchen when he was expecting a call from Buckingham Palace. The phone rang and he yelled "Get out of the way" as he clambered frantically for the handset, "that's the Queen's private secretary!" It wasn't. It was someone asking if he'd recently been involved in an accident that wasn't his fault.

On this first day of the millennium I'm expecting much the same. I ask him how he saw in the new year.
"I drank a small bottle of fizz on my own and decided I've had enough of being on my own, so I'm getting married."
"Married? I didn't even know you were seeing anyone."
"Well, we've been out a couple of times. Someone I've known for a long time, but you wouldn't know her. She's eight years younger than me, I think. She's called Alwyne and she's a judge's widow."

"Well you're a dark horse."

He carries on, oblivious: "Yes, I've decided we will get engaged on the same day I was engaged to your mother, and hopefully we'll get married on the same day too. You needn't worry though, we won't be having children as she's had a hysterectomy." My father is 75, making my prospective stepmother, 67. I wonder rapidly why on earth he would think I need that information, unless it's his way of trying to brag that he's been having some nookie. There's a brief pause while I let the full horror of the image play in my head.

"Er, oh, are you sure that's the best idea, the whole same date thing?" I think it's best to let the hysterectomy comment pass, unreferenced.

"Yes, I think it's the best plan."

"Oh OK" I say, thinking *it's a completely barmy plan you weird old man.* "Well, congratulations! I look forward to meeting her." And then he tells me that he's got a lunch coming up in a couple of days attended by the Duke of Kent, then a dinner for the Worshipful Company of Carpetbeaters & Vacuumers at the Guildhall, a committee meeting of the Commission for Aldermen's Nosegays followed by the City Commoners And Uncommoners' dinner for the annual Dipping of the Swans, then it's the Lord Mayor's Breakfast for the Counting of The Tower Ravens... and I'm flipping through the pages of a magazine until he comes to a final stop. I try to tell him about my stay in Cologne but he's not listening or it's of no interest to him whatsoever, fair enough, and we hang up.

A month later I meet Alwyne, my father's fiancee-to-be. In the meantime my father, under advisement from various members of my mother's family, has modified his grand plan for synchronising his second wife's marriage info with his first wife's and they are planning a July wedding. He has taken to calling Alwyne his "cunning little vixen" because of her red hair. I'm genuinely surprised that he is remotely aware of Janacek's opera - he certainly has never seen it - while simultaneously feeling a little nauseated by his teenagery infatuation. Other things he has revealed: she has a son by her first marriage who was raised by her second husband (the deceased judge), she's "yachty", she cooks, she paints, she lives in her house in France and in a flat in Tooting. She sounds interesting.

Our first meeting is nervous but convivial. This should work out fine. She isn't quite as arty as my father has made her out to be. She mostly paints good old-fashioned watercolours and is contemptuous of anything contemporary. She rails against a Bill Viola installation that I've just enjoyed. "Anyone could do that!" she scoffs, usually a first sign of trouble. Her yachting experience - a bit of a deal-breaker for my father I would have thought, given his love for his own boat in Cowes - amounts to a sailing holiday in the Mediterranean when she was in her twenties. I wonder too how she'll manage, holed up in the floating caravan my father adores as it grinds its way across the choppy Solent. But I'm willing to give her the benefit of the doubt.

During the spring, my father announces (announcements are very much his thing) that when they marry he's going to put the family home in Alwyne's name. Assuming he dies first, the understanding will be that in due course the house will be split three ways between my brother Nick, me and Alwyne's son David. David is married with two children. It slightly jars that David now has a stake on the house we grew up in, but it's my father's decision to make, not mine, and if it means he's happy and content, then fine. It was only to be expected. Though, we note that there's no reciprocal arrangement whereby Nick and I get a share of her French pad and the flat in Tooting. My father also says that the contents of the house will come immediately to Nick and me. I point out that this seems an odd arrangement; it will mean that his widow could well be living in a house where she owns none of the furniture.

But then, my father has never been good at owning furniture or property. He's certainly never bought any, so it doesn't seem to mean anything to him. As well as the house in Knightsbridge, over the years my grandfather has bestowed onto him an impressive and valuable portfolio: his house in Frinton-on-Sea, a thatched cottage in Wiltshire where he retired, and a flat next to Hyde Park that was his last home in London. All of these my father has sold, one after the other, to pay for what we are never quite sure. My guess is his boat.

Come the wedding day I'm in the midst of working in Munich. I fly to London, sing *Panis Angelicus,* eat plate-loads of canapes, and fly back to Bavaria again that evening. (A side note here to all prospective nuptialists: if you want

143

a singer to feel nice and detached from your wedding, ask them to sing at it, because it's no longer a wedding, it's a gig, and a gig is a gig. For the entire ceremony they'll worry how they'll do and little else.)

A week or so later I am back home and my father and Alwyne are honeymooning in a hotel nearby. They ask me over for dinner. And that's when I detect some tension for the first time. She announces she has plans for building work on the family house. First of all, she's going to have the rotting kitchen replaced. "Hallelujah" I cry, "about time too!" My father can't really see why it might be necessary. His first wife managed all right. Alwyne becomes tetchy.

"And you'll have to pay for it too" she says.

"It's your house, you pay for it!" he responds. This doesn't go down well. She looks ready to spit.

"I gave you all those shares. Sell them and pay for it!" he adds. (Shares? What shares?)

The temperature in the hotel restaurant drops below zero, which is surprising for August.

Shortly after, Lucy and I go to Cowes to spend a couple of days on my father's boat which is still moored in the same spot where my mother fell from the pontoon and died.[5]As we arrive my father is returning from the jewellers. He has

---

[5] As related in *Who's My Bottom?* After she was discovered floating at sea, my father booked a diver to search for anything she might have dropped as she fell into the marina. The diver brought up my mother's handbag and an unopened bottle of whisky. The cash in her purse was exactly the right amount for the diver's fee, and my father gave him the bottle of whisky as a tip. She had it all covered.

had a glittery, yachty brooch made for Alwyne, an exact replica of one my mother used to wear. Not to overstate it, but it's all feeling a bit odd.

Alwyne is short with us, distant, though we aren't sure why. We take the boat out for a sail and some mackerel fishing. She spends the short trip at the bow end, being sea sick, hating every minute. It turns out she's about as yachty as a Guernsey cow.

My father announces he's going to sell some family paintings to pay for the work on the kitchen that he thinks Alwyne should pay for. These are paintings that have been inherited from my mother's family. The only "art" I'm aware that my father has ever bought are a portrait of himself and a portrait of his boat.

One of the paintings he plans to sell is a very large nautical canvas that was promised to Nick (now living in California) years ago, the biggest painting in the house. Nick and I decide to write to our father, to persuade him not to sell off the family stuff, when there are better ways to raise the cash needed for work on the house, a mortgage perhaps, tiny compared to the house's value. A mortgage is surely the common-sense solution, what most people would choose. I also take the opportunity to point out that his bequeathment arrangement for the house is a bit vague. It's all very well having "an understanding" that the house will eventually be split three ways, but after he dies, Alwyne could be entitled to change her mind, and that might not be what he wants.

I think it's fair to say that this is when the shit well-and-truly hits the fan.

My father reads the letter to Alwyne and, we are told, she is furious that we are accusing her of being a gold-digger. He also says that he has never had a mortgage, which prompts the silent reply from me *well, bully for you*!, and he's "not about to start having one now". So, to the dismay of Nick, he sells his heirloom. The other painting, a naval skirmish during the Napoleonic Wars, he passes on to me because the auctioneers tell him he won't get much for it. Besides, one of Alwyne's own watercolours can hang in its place.

In anticipation of a clear-out before they start work on the kitchen, I ask for some of my mother's cooking paraphernalia, things I'll never probably never use but of which I'm fond, like a copper salmon mousse mould that has always hung on the wall.

"Why on earth do you want THAT?" asks Alwyne, frostily.

"Because it was my mother's" is my reply. She looks bemused.

At the Concertgebouw in Amsterdam, after a performance of Henze's *Elegy for Young Lovers* that I've just sung with Olly Knussen at the helm, there's a party. Henze and Fausto, our Knightsbridge neighbours, are there. Fausto wants to gossip and he draws me aside. First he tells me how sorry he is that my mother has died.

Then: "I have met your father's new wife, and you know what she told me? She says to me that she would not marry him unless he put the house in her name! Can you imagine?" and he makes a face, a face that tells me he wouldn't trust her as far as he could throw her.

I shrug. "What can I do?" He shrugs back, but clearly he thinks something fishy is afoot.

The kitchen is done and shortly afterwards, we discover that my father has been banished from the marital bedroom "because of his snoring". He starts to sleep in "the nursery", the room my brother and I slept in as children. Alwyne alone occupies the bedroom my parents used to share. He also sells his beloved boat, Lady Libby, named after my mother, who often used to joke that if she went first, he would fall "into the arms of a black widow spider." It's beginning to look like my mother knew what she was talking about.

Less than four years after they were married, when my father shows some early signs of dementia, Alwyne announces she wants a separation. My father starts to look for somewhere to live and I persuade him to move close to us in Wiltshire. We help him find a flat in a retirement complex. She, meanwhile, has her eyes on a house in Clapham. She sells the Knightsbridge house, now hers by law and worth just shy of a million pounds. My father's flat costs £175,000, the first home he has ever paid for. She pockets the balance and somehow gets him to hand over a substantial chunk of his depleted share portfolio to boot. He is becoming easily confused, unable to see what's happening, and he agrees to anything she demands. Nick and I are kept in the dark about any negotiations.

I help my father move into his small flat. Alwyne is there too, and the atmosphere is chilly. The moving van disgorges its contents but almost none of it is familiar. It isn't our family furniture, it's hers. And much of it is barely better than junk.

Notably missing is a chest of drawers, an inlaid Dutch commode, that my mother had always singled out as something she wanted to stay in the family. It isn't particularly valuable as far as I know, and it's in shoddy condition. A leg once fell off, no doubt weakened by woodworm, and my father, ever one to take proper care care of antiques, stuck it back on with a gob of UHU. My mother used to go on and on about the Dutch commode. "I'm leaving it you in my will!" she would say to whomever admired it most. It had originally come to London, like much of the furniture in the house, from her family home in Scotland.

I ask Alwyne about the Dutch commode.

"That's staying with me."

"But it was my mother's!" I protest.

"Are you trying to tell me," she hisses, "that when your mother died her things didn't become your father's, to do with exactly as he wishes?!"

My father is looking weary, bemused and distressed, so I decide to tackle this later. And when I do, he says he really doesn't want any fuss. He continues to live under the delusion that everything is fine with the marriage bar the fact that she has taken nearly everything he owns and wants to live a hundred miles away. He continues to take her to City dinners where they maintain the pretence that nothing is amiss.

Over the next two years my father becomes increasingly confused and disorientated. At a meeting with his solicitor when we are arranging a power of attorney, he asks the lawyer if he has any of his money because he can't figure out where it has gone.

He is diagnosed with frontal lobe dementia but just before I am about to address his long-term care he has a stroke and is admitted to hospital. When we visit he tells my children that he is the Emperor of Japan. From hospital he is moved to a care home. I make arrangements to sell his flat to pay for his care; he has insufficient savings to cover the cost and the separation agreement his wife has made him sign absolves Alwyne of any responsibility.

My family has now christened her The Old Trout. She calls me. She is indignant that I haven't kept her informed about my father's stroke and the plan for his care, which strikes me as a bit rich. Angry and exasperated, I tell her that I will let her know where he is being put into care if, in return, she agrees to give me my mother's commode. She can also have back several of her paintings that had hung in his flat. It's a petty bargain, but I am fed up with her and her shenanigans and I want to claim one small victory. Besides it will be good to get rid of her terrible doodles. She agrees to my request and she visits him in the care home in Wootton Bassett.

I ring her to arrange a time when I can pick up the commode and return her paintings. She announces she has changed her mind, and of course I am barely surprised. In so many words I ask her how she can live with herself, knowing she has disinherited my father's children and grandchildren, taking not only the family home but also my mother's furniture. Her answer is stunning: "I have been fortunate to be married to three reasonably wealthy men. I have come to expect a certain standard of living and I see no reason why I should compromise." She once bragged to me that, stuck in a solid traffic jam on the M4, she had simply moved onto the hard shoulder and driven past - there was no way *she* was going to queue with everybody else - so I guess I should be less surprised.

She also implies that she and my father were having an affair many years before my mother's death, but I have no way of discovering if this is true or if it's an attack at my mother, which, either way, is how it sounds.

I toy with the idea of donating her third-rate paintings to a charity shop near her house in the hope that she will see them displayed where they belong, next to old Matt Monro records and beige polyester raincoats. Instead, I take them to the local dump where I have the satisfaction of hearing them being mangled by the massive waste crusher.

One day, I visit my father in his care home and I discover that one of his housemates has done a poo on the middle of a dining table. It's just sitting there, a turd on the table. As none of the staff has noticed this until I point it out, I think it's a good time to find another care home nearer us. If it's inconvenient for The Old Trout, I couldn't care less.

He dies a few months later. I sit with him during his last hour. He looks strange, lying on his side in the bed, oddly like a hairless wolfhound, his jaw long and distended. He is unconscious as his body howls for breath, his chest rattling with each gasping inhalation. He dies and a last, long wheeze escapes from his lungs. For the first time I can remember since being on the platform of Waterloo Station bound for prep school, I touch his hand, an intimacy that only death allows.

My brother Nick flies in from Los Angeles and we make funeral arrangements. I write to The Old Trout - I don't want to speak to her - and tell her he has died and that she will not be invited to any funeral. Just my brother and I attend the cremation. She writes to Nick telling him that she has arranged a memorial service in the City which she "expects us to attend". Clearly this is a ruse to play the grieving widow on his old turf, but we are having none of it. Nick replies that if she had bothered to ask she would have discovered that neither of us can make her performance as he has to be in LA and I in Milan. In his own words, he tells her to fuck off out of our lives. "I'll leave it to you to explain our absence" he writes.

We make our own arrangements for a big family send-off, a scattering of his ashes in the Solent where our mother had been scattered twelve years earlier. We drink, we eat, we cry, we laugh. We neither see nor hear from The Trout again.

Roast lamb

There's a remote corner in our wardrobe that my wife's various dresses occupy and it's where I hang my concert suits. I haven't worn my tails for four years now. This is partly because they are falling out of fashion - about time too - and partly because I don't do many concerts these days. It's a younger tenor's turn to sing all those *Masses* and *Messiahs*. I'm hoping the tails I have will see me through to retirement because, frankly, I'll be buggered if I'm buying any more. Call me stingy, but I really can't see new ones giving me enough miles to the gallon.

In forty years of singing I've only ever bought one tail suit. In my early career I was lucky enough to inherit two suits from my father and my grandfather. They came from a social class and generation for whom wearing tails to go out to dinner or the theatre was quite normal. My grandfather's tail coat had small holes in the lapel where his medals used to be pinned. He fought in the Somme, where he got shell-shock, and I thought of him particularly whenever I sang Britten's *War Requiem*. I kept wearing the coat of the jolly, gentle old man I knew, long after moths had left much bigger holes all over the fine wool fabric. It was only when the crotch of the trousers split open after decades of strenuous *Creations* that I had to give the suit up.

My newer tails are 100% polyester, shiny yet bland, and indigestible to moths. There are no medal holes. They've never been worn by anyone brave or selfless enough.

The only dinner jacket I own is white. I bought it second-hand twenty-one years ago for a concert in Macau of a mass by the Portuguese baroque composer Texeira. The conductor insisted on white tuxedos. I've never worn it since, nor sung any Texeira either. But who has? On the extremely rare occasions I'm asked to wear a black dinner jacket I just wear a black suit with a bow tie. So far, no-one has batted an eyelid. Not being a freemason, a croupier or likely ever to win an Oscar, I see no reason to buy a proper one.

Also on the rail is a morning suit of the type worn at fancy weddings. I've never worn it at a fancy wedding, only for The Bach Choir who perform the *St Matthew Passion* every year on Palm Sunday morning and who insist upon a morning suit. At least, they used to. I was their Evangelist for several years but, uncertain I would be asked back regularly, only got around to buying my own suit (rather than hiring one at great expense) after four years. I think I got about six concerts' use out if it, but if my children ever have fancy weddings, and they won't if I have any say in the matter, at least that's one less thing I'll have to worry about.

Pizza Margherita

Texas Eagle, St Louis to Chicago, 2011

I'm trying my best not to be disappointed. That's especially difficult when you haven't had much sleep. It was Lucy's final performance of *The Death of Klinghoffer* last night at the Opera Theatre of St Louis, and afterwards we went to The Tent (the marquee with a bar where cast and audience mingle after performances) so we could make our farewells. There had been the odd rumbles of distant thunder earlier in the evening but the skies were pretty clear. Within half an hour we were in the grip of a full-blown midwestern storm.

The weather in Saint Louis is unlike anything I've ever experienced before. For starters I'd never heard a tornado warning until this trip. Sirens blare and a barely intelligible voice echoes around the city telling everyone to get into their basements. With the recent news about Joplin, where hundreds died when a massive tornado touched down, a twister so fierce that it stripped the bark off trees, and seeing for myself Saint Louis airport, which had been hit at Easter and where half the windows are still boarded up with chipboard, you bet I was down in that cellar the moment that siren started wailing. Luckily no tornado landed on our neighbourhood but a few other parts of town got visited upon for a moment or two and the odd roof got stripped.

Thunderstorms seem to have a habit of whipping up in an instant. They zoom across the empty plains like vicious joyriders, smacking things around a bit for a few moments of noisy chaos, then leaving as quickly as they arrived. Last night's arrived quickly but it clearly liked beating up Saint Louis and so, unusually, it hung around for four hours. Only during a brief lull in the torrential rain were we able to escape The Tent and run to our car to drive home. At 3 a.m. the storm finally eased up and staggered off to bed, like a belligerent drunk.

We were up again at 6.15 and off to the railway station by 7. We're taking the Amtrak train, The Texas Eagle that began its journey more than a day ago in San Antonio, up to Chicago. I'm writing this on the train.

America has some fine railway stations. Washington DC's Union Station is lovely. New York's Grand Central is stunning. A pity that most useful trains go from the much duller Penn (though I would loved to have seen the old Penn Station, notoriously flattened before its destruction could be prevented). Los Angeles' Union Station is another beauty. Saint Louis used to be one of the busiest rail hubs in the country and its old Union Station reflected that - a manorial terminus built in stone. The Amtrak station has been moved and the old Union Station is now a chain hotel and third-rate shopping centre, while the new station is a steel-framed shed that makes Bristol Parkway and Watford Junction seem luxurious. Such a pity and a real downer when you've envisaged something from a 1930s movie, with a steaming station buffet-cum-oyster-bar (as you find in Grand Central), that's peopled with ticket clerks wearing green visors and sleeve bracelets, with porters wearing smart blue uniforms and beaming smiles.

Amtrak would have you believe many of these fantasies and a few others besides. For instance, they offer a free checked baggage service. We thought this would be a good idea rather than handling our four suitcases ourselves. So we rolled up good and early only to be told that the service wasn't available. We waited for a half hour in a long tetchy queue, not unlike waiting to board a Ryanair flight in the old days, and dragged our suitcases onto the train. The carriages on this route are double-decker and you leave your bags below and ride up top. Oddly, also like Ryanair of old, you have a train reservation but no reserved seat. A conductor asks you where you're headed and points you into a carriage where you look for a seat that doesn't already have a ticket above it, or a person in it, and climb in. Another conductor comes along (there are plenty of them on American trains), checks your ticket and scribbles out a reservation slip for the seats. That's you set for the rest of your journey. Now you can wander around the train or sit in the observation car (or Lounge Car as they call it).

Amtrak's blurb says this train has a dining car. You can even look at the menu online, where there are photos with smiling chefs, and tables decked with white linen tablecloths. I was up for a bit of this and last night had already punted on French toast with maple syrup, presented, so I imagined, in an elegant metal jug with Amtrak's logo on the side. And coffee in an Amtrak cup, china of course. On the white linen cloth.

We asked the conductor if the dining car was open for breakfast. "The dining car is not in operation but you can buy snacks from below the lounge". Oh. No apology or explanation. No smile. That's just the way it is, and I suspect it's the way it always is on this leg of the journey. That explained why we saw several passenger detraining at Saint Louis (where the train stops for about an hour) and popping into the station's KFC for some hot, albeit disgusting food. Yes, that's what you get instead of a steaming buffet-cum-oyster-bar: a KFC and a Pizza Hut.

As the train crawled out of Saint Louis and across the seething Mississippi I volunteered to get us some breakfast. Lucy bagged a booth in the Lounge Car and I went downstairs. The buffet made First Great Western's seem positively opulent. A guy who had clearly been to a special Amtrak clinic to have any bonhomie surgically drained from his system responded to my request for various breakfast items from the menu in a flat negative which implied I was several kinds of idiot to even ask for them.

"Two of your yoghurts please."

"There ain't any." (Thinks: what kind of moron wants yoghurt?)

I gave up scanning the menu (Bagel and Cream Cheese? Nope...Muffin? Nope...) and just ordered what I could see scattered about him. So Lucy and I each had a plastic-wrapped Sara Lee "cinnamon danish" and coffee in paper cups. It turns out the buffet guy was doing an egg, sausage and cheese muffin because someone else got one, scalding hot and still wrapped in cellophane, which can only mean it had been electrocuted in a microwave. I think I'd rather stick with the eternally "fresh" danish. Funny that, as it was trying very hard to stick to me.

Next to the Lounge we could see a Dining Car. My hackles preparing to rise, I asked a passing steward about it. "Only open to sleeper passengers" was the response. Sleeper passengers get meals included in the price of the ticket so feeding the few people I could see in there was an obligation. I couldn't see any table cloths though. Or jugs of maple syrup.

The Lounge Car is all very well with its curved ceiling windows and outside-facing seats but on this stretch of journey there is very little to look at. The countryside of Illinois is an expanse of dull farmland, mostly vast fields of corn. Otherwise it's all suburbs or, worst of all, large tracts of ruined industrial landscape. You could be forgiven for thinking, from looking out of the windows as you pass through most of these cities, that America is pretty-much broken. It's an impression that riding in its slow and inefficient trains does very little to dispel. What a pity.

No sooner had I plonked down that last full stop when something rather sweet happened. A conductor announced that there was pizza for the whole train, a slice each which we could collect from the Lounge Car. She called us in, coach by coach (there are only three coaches aside from the sleepers and the Lounge and Dining cars) and everyone took back to their seats a slice of cheese, pepperoni or sausage pizza on a plastic Amtrak plate, as well as some cookies, crackers and dried fruit. It looked like the pizzas has been delivered straight to the train at the station where we last stopped.

How very surprising, and I've no idea why they did it. Or whether this is a regular thing. "Hello, Dominos? Yes, it's the Texas Eagle. I know, again, right? So what are your specials today? And how quickly can you knock up fifty pizzas?"

I also see that we are now running alongside the old Route 66. Things are looking up. And for just $32 (£20) each for a ticket it seems churlish of me to complain.

Corned Beef Hash

There are many misconceptions that hang around the neck of contemporary opera. I'm not going to try to address them all. It would make for a tedious read and besides, my experience, like all experiences, is individual. If I were to lay down a treatise on "how it is to do contemporary opera" somebody else would, rightly, come along and disagree with me. So, I'll modify my first sentence and pretty-well every sentence in this chapter by leaving an imaginary "in my experience", unwritten but implied, before everything I have to say about it.

I've done a dozen brand new operas - world premieres - and lots of nearly-new ones in various national premieres. Of the new operas, I'd say only one of the operas could be counted as a major success, both critically and at the box office. Some won awards, a few were televised, and about a third of them have gone on to be produced for a second time; though I strongly suspect that had more to do with reasons other than the quality of the work. It can hardly come as a surprise that of all the factors involved in achieving success for an opera, the quality of the opera alone might not be the most crucial element in its success. Some of the new operas I've done have been star vehicles - not for me, I hasten to add - and the measure of their success had less to do with how well they served "art" and more to do with how well they showcased their lead protagonists. Nothing new there. If these operas had shortcomings, they could be ignored as long as the stars got to show off their considerable skills.

Perhaps - tending as I do to play second fiddle rather than first in the operatic scheme of things - this is why I can say I have rarely collaborated at all with any of the composers. But I'm not sure that's the only reason.

Commissioning an opera is a long, slow process. I say this with the limited experience of being a director of a small arts organisation that commissions new music. When a butcher makes sausages, by the time the sausages are stuffed into their skins and ready for sale it's usually too late for collaboration with the people who are eventually going to stick them in a pan and cook them. If you want to have a bigger say in the way the sausages are made, you should probably take up working in an abattoir. (Other food analogies are available. Growing the potatoes that end up as crisps would do just as well, for the vegans amongst us.)

More often than not, by the time I have been cast, the vocal score has been published and printed, and it's too late for big amendments. Like singing Bach or Wagner, it's the singer's job to sing exactly what's on the page, not rewrite it willy-nilly. Some composers - quite a lot in fact - have a limited understanding of the voice and, say, because they've heard a tenor should have a top C, will write loads and loads of them as if all the tenor has to do is plonk them out on an instrument. Faced with a score like that, my reaction would be to say I'm unsuitable and withdraw. Or some sort of compromise has to be reached. I've never seen that situation get ugly. Usually, the composer backs down, admits his shortcomings and modifications are made. Though why no-one further up the commissioning process hasn't spotted the shortcomings and said something leaves pause for reflection. Could it be that the people who are doing the commissioning are also not that clued-up on what makes for a singable opera and what doesn't?

Only recently, for the first time that I can remember, was I sent a score ahead of publication; for perusal and with the option to request changes if I wanted them. I'll admit that all I did was scan through the score and check that it didn't have any notes that are completely beyond my reach. That's not to say that there aren't some notes that I'd prefer not to sing (see the paragraph above), but I'll do them if I must and as infrequently as possible. I like a bit of a challenge, sometimes, and it does one no harm to take the difficult option and overcome it, rather than make the whole role a bit of a doddle. And besides, there are quite enough roles in the rest of the repertoire that cause us to shit bricks. Why should new ones be any different? Shitting bricks and getting on with it all the same is what separates the professionals from the amateurs.

Composers tend to show up to rehearsals for their new operas and say absolutely nothing to the singers. They smile nervously and appreciatively, as if they can't believe someone has taken what they've written and is actually singing it, sitting there aghast with gratitude that you're trying your best to get it right, even though you might be getting chunks of it wrong. Apparently even Benjamin Britten was like this. When his acolytes pointed out wrong notes that his singers were delivering he would even defend the singers: "Oh it's terribly difficult that bit" or "I think he is singing that passing note, just so quickly you can't hear it." Incidentally, while we have Britten in the witness stand, it is worth pointing out that he never thought of his world premiere performances as the finished product. He frequently made substantial changes afterwards. They were considered "works in progress". This is something that happens rarely these days and I'm not sure why.

Some composers have struck me as tone deaf. Either they can't remember what it is they were trying to write, or they don't actually know if what we're singing is right or wrong. Sometimes they're so depressed by what the director has chosen to do with their masterpiece that they spend the whole rehearsal period looking pale and sad.

I have asked composers if they're happy with what I'm doing and, bar one, they have said "yes", with that slightly terrified expression of "why are you asking me?"
The one composer who thought he could add a bit more took me off to a small room and tried to demonstrate how he imagined a long stretch of *sprechstimme* should go. This, I should add, was a long passage, a soliloquy, that had been added very late to the rest of the score. The ink was barely dry when I got it.

Sprechstimme is a mixed bag. It is often written with specific pitches, even though you're speaking rather than singing, but generally it is acceptable to be close to pitch rather than bang in the middle of it, given you're not really participating in conventional harmony. The most important skill, I think, is to replicate the shape of the phrase the composer has set down rather than worrying whether you should be saying, say, "arse" on an A-flat as opposed to an A-double-flat. And if you're wondering, the chances are that if you're doing *sprechstimme*, "arse" is a word you will have to say/sing somewhere along the line.

This composer, the one who wanted to demonstrate the *sprechstimme,* could only hit the right pitches if he played along on the piano, a luxury unavailable to me on stage. So I immediately stopped worrying as to whether he was noticing any mistakes on my part, because he clearly couldn't hear them without a piano to refer to. Having discarded that concern, I listened to him perform his own soliloquy. It was terrible. As I nodded and chewed my lip while he gurgled his way through the passage, I calmly decided that I certainly wasn't going to do it like that. I thanked him profusely for his help and did it my way from thereon. He was terribly pleased with the result.

If there's a moral to that tale it is that often you have to remind yourself that composers, locked away in solitary rooms for months on end, are more than likely to have terrible theatrical instincts. It's the singer's job to sing their notes - yes, obviously - *and* to turn what are often half-baked ideas into fully iced cakes with candles on top. Sometimes that means ignoring them a little bit.

I like doing new operas for the same reasons that all the singers I know like doing them. You hope to find *that* role. The one that ticks all the boxes, musically and dramatically, and which people are seeing without any preconceptions of how it should go. The audience isn't comparing your performance to a long line of previous incumbents in the role; you're all they've got to go on. It's the same for actors in plays and movies. Though it is a trait most strongly seen in opera, the habit of repeating over and over again the same repertoire, in the same roles. Only the rarest of Shakespearean actors gets to do the big roles in more than one production. Opera singers do it all the time.

Despite the quirks of opera, I don't think there's any difference to the way you approach a new role, whether it has been done a million times before or whether you are its first protagonist. If you learn a new role by copying how someone else has done it, then I really don't know what to say. I don't know if I'm odd that way, but when I'm doing a new "standard" role, I avoid listening to recordings of other singers doing it, unless I'm in a massive hurry and need a recording as a learning aid. So, the note-bashing at the piano, the research, the being up half the night fretting about how to sing and play someone... it's all the same, new music or old.

Pedigree Chum

(In 2012 I gave a short lecture called "You Can't Win" to a room full of young singers. This is most of what I said:)

When I was asked to do this, I had an idea of what I'd like to talk to you about and came up with a catchy title, little thinking how stupid it would sound in the midst of Olympic fever when most of us are thinking about nothing but winning. But bear with me. This isn't an exercise in cynicism. Some time in the future, if it hasn't happened already, you will find yourself alone in a distant hotel room, in a pre-performance purgatory, asking yourself this question: "what's it all about?" I hope then you'll remember some of what I've said today.

There's probably a good reason why you're here today. You want to find out some secrets to success. You feel that, a lot of the time, you can't get a break. You're banging your head against a brick wall. You go for auditions but most of them aren't productive. Other singers in your generation are getting on but you feel you just can't win.
You may be entering lots of competitions at the moment, and while you may do pretty well, you're finding it hard to take home the prizes. You may even have friends who are cleaning up and while you're pleased for them, there's also a bit of you that is thinking "it's just not fair!"
Now, I'm not here to tell you whether the music business is fair or not. I can reassure you that there is a vast number of working singers who have never, ever won a prize. And

every singer I know will tell you horror stories about disastrous auditions and embarrassing performances. The main reason I'm here and why I've chosen this apparently cynical title - You Can't Win - is because I firmly believe that the sooner a singer understands that you really can't win, the better and happier singer he or she will be.

This is something I've wrestled with all my singing life. I don't know how many of you have read my book *Who's My Bottom?* but in it I describe my own struggle (and it's one which I think is recognisable to any professional singer) with understanding what success means as a singer, and the vast chasm that exists between the perception of what a singing career is like and the often brutal reality.

In the book I quote a story about my old singing teacher and friend Bob Tear. A very famous bass said to him; "You know, Bob, my ambition is to be the best bass in the world." To which Bob replied; "That's lovely, dear. But how will you know?"

Only recently I visited the website of a young tenor whom I'd seen in a show in Paris. The website declared him to be "the most successful tenor of his generation". Ironically, I can't remember his name, but as Bob would have said: how could he possibly know?

Now, I understand how hype works but what disturbs me about both these singers is that they clearly regard being a singer as one eternal competition that one day they can win. Yes, it's competitive, but when I say You Can't Win, I want to tell you that being singer is not a race. There is no finishing line. You really can't win because being a singer isn't about winning. And if the only reason you want to be a singer is to beat everyone else and prove something, then somewhere down the line I think you will become horribly unstuck.

I was thinking of a way to illustrate this and the best I can come up with is a greyhound race. I don't know if any of you has ever been to a greyhound race; I haven't but I'm sure we all know how they work. A mechanical hare whizzes past the starting cages, the hounds are released and they basically chase the hare around the track in a contest that lasts barely a minute. From the punter's point of view, yes, there is a winner - the first past the finishing post - and the lucky punter counts his winnings. But let's just look at this from the greyhound's point of view. The greyhound's goal was to catch the elusive hare, but in this it always fails, as the furry machine zips away into the distance. The dog has no concept of a finishing line. It means nothing to the dog, only to the punter. All the dog walks away with for its efforts is an extra meaty-flavoured treat.

Generally I'd say that in our business, it's the so-called "gatekeepers" who approach our business from the point of view of the punters at a racecourse. They want winners. They take a gamble. That's how they see the employment of us. Meanwhile, we singers and performers are the greyhounds. We may be declared the winners or a safe bet by the punters (for as long as we can actually win races) but if we are not careful we will end up eternally chasing something that is forever elusive, and all just for a few meaty-tasting morsels. From a greyhound's point of view, you can't win.

Far from being depressed by this, I find the realisation that you can't win to be very releasing. Don't get me wrong; I'm not dissuading you from being the best singer you can be, I'm just warning you that if your only aim in life is to beat your colleagues, you'll never achieve your goal. Far better, I'd say, and continuing the sporting theme, to spend your career looking forward and enjoying the physical thrill of running than be constantly looking over your shoulder to see how the competition is doing.

I also think the You Can't Win philosophy works in performance. We've all been in shows where so-and-so, perhaps it was even you, "stole the show" - emerged as the clear winner, if you like. Quite apart from the fact that this is often as much to do with the role as the performer (let's face it - how many times does Tamino win the affections of an audience over Papageno?) - as often as not, you will find yourselves singing roles where you simply cannot "win". This is where I would urge you to recognise that our job is not to suck up to the audience and try to win their affections. Our job is to be as honest and truthful to our role as we possibly can. It isn't to seek the love of the punters. A punter's love is fickle, as easily lost as won. Never, ever confuse having a successful career, full of plaudits from the public and critics, having their love, with having a private life or anything approaching a proper relationship.

Personally I've often found it much more enjoyable to play anti-heroes, losers, difficult and weird individuals, as opposed to "winners" - good guys - simply because I'm not burdened with any worry about being appealing. I can simply get on with my job, sing and play a character. I know I can't "win", so I'm going to enjoy myself in the pure pleasure of performing.

The other problem with an attitude of having to win a performance is that it again implies that for you to win, your colleagues must lose. And at what cost? I remember a famous tenor describing to me how he had decided that a young soprano he was working with was doing far too good a job for his liking - in rehearsal she was showing him up - so he had gone on stage with the intention of "blowing her out of the water" and delighted in telling me that this is what he had subsequently done. He told me this story as if I should admire his panache, but in truth I found it rather sad. To me he sounded like someone who had forgotten why he had become a singer in the first place. And as successful as he was, he always struck me as a troubled and dissatisfied man who never felt he got his just desserts.

Apart from all those bloody competitions that singers have to do these days, what else drives the misguided urge to win? When I was your age I remember all too well that I felt an enormous need to prove my success to my parents and I'm sure I'm not alone in that. In fact that need only dissipated once my parents had died.

"How's it going?" they would ask. And I would feel this overwhelming burden not to disappoint them. It was a huge thing. If I didn't have news of good offers and stuff I could brag about I was sure I could hear them thinking "Oh dear, perhaps this singing lark wasn't such a good idea after all." If you don't suffer from this sort of pressure then good for you, but if you do, the best cure is to take them out to dinner and pick up the bill. That shuts them up.

So, learn that, for all the competing you are having to do now, there is no real finishing line, no winning post. That way lies nothing but the prospect of Pedigree Chum treats to keep you happy. Enjoy your music making for what it is now, at the very moment you make it, not for where it puts you in "the rankings" or for how it will advance your career. Success in our business is measured ultimately by your ability to pay your bills. There really is no greater or more significant achievement than that.

Fish Fingers

If you asked me why there is so much opera for children going on at the moment, I would honestly have to say I don't know. Usually, in the costly world I work in, it's a good idea to take the *All The President's Men* lead and "follow the money". So, my guess is that there is gold in them thar hills. Sorry, that sounds cynical. I'm sure the intention of getting young people into opera is absolutely sincere - and indeed it is praiseworthy - but I'll bet there's a tasty chunk of extra Arts Council funding for it too.

Does putting on so-called children's opera encourage them to stick with the tricky genre as they become adults? Difficult to say, but there's probably no harm in trying; though I don't understand the logic whereby a performance which is a bit of a trial for adults - I'm remembering a particularly third-rate *Magic Flute* I saw a couple of years ago - is supposed to be good enough for children. Like young noses, *Magic Flutes* should be picked carefully.

Some of the current crop of youth-friendly operas have a lot of kids in them. But I'm dubious about the idea that an opera with lots of children in it is more likely to appeal to kids than one without. Even as a child, the bits I always found least interesting in *any* form of entertainment were the bits with kids in, and that includes *Mary Poppins* and *The Sound of Music.* And that hasn't changed as I've supposedly grown up. Much as I adore Britten's music, there's too often the *de rigeur* bit where some kids sing and I want it to be over as soon as possible; the chorus of midshipmen in *Billy Budd* being a cringe-worthy case in point.

From a promoter's point of view, the main benefit of a child-heavy cast is the guarantee that you'll sell at least two tickets for every child in the show. A lot more if the grandparents come too.

With my own children - now in their late twenties and partial to the occasional bit of opera - I don't ever remember taking them to a "children's opera". They came to a few rehearsals and saw their dad doing the usual things like being stabbed in the neck, and prancing around like an idiot ("...and that, my little sausages, is what pays the mortgage...") and we saw a production of *Carmen* in Cologne that was pure *regietheater*. They didn't bat an eyelid. And I don't think they became particularly interested when the children's chorus appeared. If anything, my adolescent son was more focussed on the Carmen's cleavage, my teenage daughter, on a handsome dancer with good legs.

This isn't to say there aren't some brilliant "children's operas" - Oliver Knussen's *Where The Wild Things Are* and *Higglety Pigglety Pop!* being, for me, particularly outstanding as they are musically uncompromising, <u>and</u> performed entirely by adults; unlike some of Britten's (*Let's Make An Opera* for instance) which are full of kids and can get rather twee. For a long time I've longed for someone to write an all-adult opera of *Billy Bunter*.

Alice in Wonderland has now had so many versions that I wonder if it's time to call a moratorium on any more. For ten years. I'm not even sure it's a children's piece. So much of it is baffling. I've sung in two versions and I'd struggle to explain the plot of either.

No, I'd say the winning formula for converting children to opera is to make sure it's properly done, to the very highest standard. Do it well and they'll get it. Don't do something with a trombone, a cello and a clown and expect it to produce masses of converts to classical music. It was a child, after all, who pointed at the Emperor and announced loudly that he was wearing no clothes.

Tyco the Vegan

At last it can be revealed, in classic British synopsis styling: Benjamin Britten's contemplated space-age opera, as mentioned in biographies by Humphrey Carpenter and Paul Kildea: *TYCO THE VEGAN*.

Prologue

An intergalactic truth and reconciliation event. Tyco (his skin is scaly and green, he has four eyes) is on trial (but in a non-judgmental way) for eating a pork sausage. His defence: it slipped into his mouth by accident.

Act 1

Space interlude 1: The Soya Milky Way On Mars a chorus of Martian vegans and boys greets the sunrise with yoga and Tai Chi. Tyco lands his flying saucer with a massive crate of tofu, but he is shunned. Only Thesbia of Venus stands by him, as well as Cap'n Birdseye from Earth. Findus of Murco tells Tyco he has secured him a fresh supply of veggie sausages but the Martians suspect his veracity and are outraged in a strictly non-violent way. There is a meteor storm, during which Tyco tells Birdseye of his ambitions of opening a

175

falafel chain across the galaxy: "I dream of making it big in Uranus".

Space Interlude 2: Meteor Storm
Night time (which lasts 38 hours) in the co-operative inn: "The Chia Seed and Soybean". The nettle wine is flowing. Tyco has come to meet Findus and collect his sausages. Tyco sings the aria "My Satnav always mistakes the Great Bear for Extragallacticon 13". A drinking song ensues: "Old Jo has gone looking for sustainable quinoa". Tyco collects his sausages and leaves for his flying saucer. The act ends with the line: "Inter-Planetary Transportation Device! Do you call that an IPTD?!"

Act 2

Space interlude 3: Argon Morning
It is morning on Argon, the seventh sun in the Iphoxian galaxy, and the Martians are at the Deodrome, all except Thesbia who is boiling chickpeas. Tyco appears. He wants to take the chickpeas to his IPTD and zoom to Jupiter. The Jupitans are having a music festival and Tyco sees his opportunity to start his falafel empire. A row ensues and Tyco storms off. A mob gathers and they decided to head to Tyco's IPTD to check it for meat.

Passacaglia.

Scene: Tyco's spaceship, his IPTD. Whilst deep-frying his falafel and contemplating his future with Thesbia, Tyco stumbles on the unopened box of Findus's sausages. Peeling off an outer label he sees that the sausages are in fact pork bangers. As the mob approaches, some fall into the deep fat fryer and in order to hide the evidence, Tyco gorges himself on sausages. He steps into the Matter Transpodulator and disappears, just in time. Finding no sausages in the ship, the mob disperses. Cap'n Birdseye remains and finds the discarded label.

Act 3

Space Interlude 4: Like, Peace, Man. Scene: Desmond Tutu Community and Peace Centre. A "Recycling Awareness Freeform Celebration of World Dance (Bring Your Own Bongo Drums)" is taking place. Rumours start to spread that uneaten meat sausages and piles of boiled chickpeas have been found in a crater just a few steps from Tyco's IPTD. Again a mob forms, intent on raising a petition and having a cruelty awareness day. They leave and Thesbia is left to sing her aria "Native American Dreamcatchers are, like, so spiritual".

Scene: A crater. Tyco is half-mad and sings a soliloquy. Cap'n Birdseye discovers him and tells him to fly his spaceship into the galaxy and open the hatch. Next morning. The vegans of Mars go about their daily business, cleaning their yurts and polishing their tantric crystals, while an IPTD drifts ever deeper into space.

Roast turkey

Utter incredulity seemed to be the reaction, just a few years ago, when a video of Stephane Lissner, artistic director of the Paris Opera, revealed himself unable to identify some of the most popular operas in the repertoire, *Carmen* and *Madama Butterfly* included.

Was the reaction incredulity? Or perhaps it was resignation?

I'm quite sure there would be plenty of other opera bosses who would be equally stumped. I know I would be if we strayed into certain corners of the operatic canon. But on reflection I think the surprising thing is that we expect the people who lead opera companies to have a background in opera, when experience should surely have taught us by now that this is rarely the case.

Oh sure, some of them will have worked in opera houses for quite a while, learning the ropes on their way up the greasy pole, but I bet I could count on the fingers of one hand the number who are musicians in any shape or form. I've certainly met very few who can actually read a score. Perhaps that isn't an absolute necessity, but much as I adore cricket I wouldn't dream of applying to captain a cricket team, as the last time I looked I discovered that I have absolutely no cricketing skills whatsoever beyond shouting "oh, well played!" from time to time. But it would be reassuring to know that the people who hire and fire you have at least <u>some</u> basic skills in your area of work, rather than garnering everything they know from CD booklets and PR handouts.

I've had first-hand experience of this. A casting director, now an *intendant*, had doubts that I might be suitable for a modern piece because he'd been told it was written for a Rossini tenor. I suggested we have a look at the score together, which was like reading Tolstoy with a toddler. He could barely read music. And, surprise surprise, the score revealed that the role was about as Rossinian as a bag of tadpoles.

Off the top of my head, I can count amongst prominent opera artistic leaders a few stage directors, a lawyer, some PR managers, a couple of accountants, some TV executives, an ex-clarinettist, several ex-administrators and a record executive. There's one working singer and two ex-singers, that's all. And one conductor.

I don't expect this will change anytime soon, if ever, and I'm sure someone can come up with a myriad of reasons why artistic policy is best put in the hands of so many non-artists. And I'm not trying to say that opera houses *shouldn't* be run by people who are good at accountancy, wearing suits and staying in good hotels on business expenses. But before anybody insists it *has* to be this way, I would point out that by contrast, straight theatres are almost exclusively run by practitioners of the art form; actors and directors. So there.

Cold chicken

Ah, summer! Lazy afternoons in the sun, gardens abundant with flowers and fruit, picnics on the grass with chilled champagne, and lots and lots of opera sung in the open air. I'm not sure why it is, but the British - with our notoriously wonderful rain-free summers, our abundant love for opera sung in all those foreign languages we speak so well, and our tendency to bouts of sarcasm - will jump at any chance to get outdoors and bung on an opera on an un-canopied, makeshift stage. It's almost a national disease. At the first sign of sunshine in April, the entire nation rushes to the DIY store to buy barbecues and patio furniture, and many of them to the online box office to book tickets for open-air opera, happily forgetting meanwhile how last year's summer was ruined by flooding and record low temperatures.

I've sung outdoors often; in Italy - no problem, Greece - not a cloud in the sky, France - never a drop of rain, but England? Are we sure this is a good idea?

In the early days of Garsington Opera, near Oxford, before they came to their senses and built a seasonal theatre, I sang *Cosi fan Tutte* under an open sky. Words cannot describe the horror of singing *Un aura amorosa* with absolutely no acoustic, while planes fly overhead in an increasingly greying sky. A neighbour's lawnmower accompanied the orchestra, nearby dogs howled - in appreciation no doubt - and a chilly wind hurled through my gauzy Neapolitan costume. Maintaining an expression of loving awe with that lot going on was one of the great achievements of my career. When we performed the last act finale through a steady drizzle, our wigs matting on our faces, the orchestra toiling away under a plastic sheet, Garsington's management realised that steps had to be taken. The next year they built an elegant canopy, but it only covered the audience and pit.

I was back there a few years later to sing Leukippos in Richard Strauss's *Daphne.* I was dressed only in a loincloth (just for a change) and when Apollo felled me with his arrow, I had to lie all-but-naked for twenty minutes after my death, long after the sun had gone down, while Daphne sang her long final lament and the opera ended. Some nights this was fine, but on most I had to summon all my will to stop my body shaking with cold. Take it from me, it's not a skill they teach you at conservatoire. If the audience was oblivious to the cold - they certainly were to the fact that Leukkipos was slowly turning blue - it was because in the years since my last appearance, Garsington had installed central heating under the seats of the temporary auditorium. Again, nothing for the stage. All that could spoil a punter's enjoyment now was a soggy picnic and the sound of torrential rain beating down on the auditorium roof. Oh, and the planes, dogs and lawnmowers. As for the singers, as long as we avoided catching pneumonia, we were happy.

Wilted Spinach

2015

Opera singers have a reputation for being far too occupied with money. This has often struck me as unfair, not least because I've always found conductors, despite the holier-than-thou image they tend to manufacture ("I'm only interested in the MUSIC"), to be much greedier. Just look at the enormous fees they earn for making absolutely no sound beyond the occasional intrusive grunt. Just look at the massive salaries they are paid for part-time directorships of multiple orchestras and opera houses.

But my gripe today isn't with conductors. It's with opera companies who don't pay their singers on time. Note that I say *singers*, because it has always been my experience that the conductor always gets paid, no matter what happens. Only recently, the Rome Opera failed to pay some of their lowest-earning singers on time - money they needed to feed their families - while promptly handing over a vast amount of money to the conductor who was meanwhile collecting a million-dollar salary in the USA. They could have paid *all* the singers completely and it still would have made only a smallest of dents in the conductor's paycheck, so massive was the difference in their fees. What the conductor needed the money for in such a hurry is anyone's guess. Hair products, probably.

In Florence, the Maggio Musicale is up to its old tricks. Despite having built an expensive new theatre, it seems their budget doesn't run to paying performers to sing in it.

Social media is awash with singers complaining they haven't been paid, some for operas as far back as 2013. In May of 2015 they put on four performances of *Candide,* but at the end of October they have still only paid the singers for ONE performance. The one fee may have just about covered the singers' expenses - their flights and accommodation - but probably not. All pleas to be paid are greeted with excuses like: "Everyone is on holiday, next month maybe..." and "We just don't have the money right now." Or the pleas are simply ignored. But I assume the people making the excuses are collecting their substantial salaries. They can afford to go on holiday after all, unlike the singers whose livelihood they are denying.

Imagine engaging a self-employed contractor to build you a flashy new kitchen, with marble surfaces, top-of-the range appliances...even an American fridge and a built-in cappuccino machine. You draw up a contract. He builds your kitchen, supplying all the materials and appliances on the understanding that you will pay him when it's done. And then you say "Oh, I'm sorry, I can't pay you because I'm going away on holiday. Perhaps sometime next year?"

Now imagine being the man who has built the kitchen. For any singers reading this, my advice is: whatever you do, don't build any kitchens for the Maggio Musicale.

Black Pudding

Today it was a pair of black socks. A few weeks ago it was the woman in the bar. Both presented me with what I like to call an existential crisis, but which might be better called a massive, depressing bout of self-evaluation.

Let's start with the socks.

It would be easy to argue there aren't many blessings to be found - financially anyway - in a life spent being self-employed and working in the arts. Heck, I've spent the last decade or so running that very idea as a cottage industry, writing the sort of stuff I'm writing right now. Chief among its blessings - besides, yes I know, <u>getting to make lovely music</u> (I have to say that or the people who don't actually understand that <u>can be taken as a given</u> tend to get their knickers in a twist) - is the lack of a dress code.

Well, alright, there's a dress code when you have to put on all the fancy evening dress stuff, including black socks, for concerts, but for all the other hours in the year, you can wear pretty-much what you like. And for me, for most of the year, I open my sock drawer - which, for the sake of full disclosure also houses underpants, hankies, cufflinks, pyjamas, a couple of ties pushed to the back, a redundant ruby red cummerbund, and quite a lot of loose foreign change - and I can choose between an array of socks of many different and garish colours. This isn't because I see the wearing of coloured socks as an essential manifestation of my character but because it's easier to pair up socks after they've been washed when you can figure out which sock goes with which on a straightforward pink-goes-with-pink, blue-goes-with-blue basis.

With black socks this has never been my strong suit. They're so difficult to match up. The black socks that greet me this morning are a case in point. I'm not convinced they're really a pair. They might have been identical twins once, but separation over the decades - we are talking about seriously old socks - has meant that the individual socks are less black and more different shades of dark grey. The elastic at the cuff looks different. They <u>look</u> terribly small too. Did they fit my once more slender feet better than they do now? And the fact that they were black meant that I bought them to wear for concerts. What did I sing in these socks? Where have they travelled? On what concert platforms, in which cathedrals, have they stood while I warbled? It's not impossible that they're not my socks at all. They could be my wife's, which would explain the smallness.

I almost throw away the pair of blackish socks. They haven't worn through yet but they are on the cusp. These are probably the last remaining survivors of a whole drawerful of black socks that have slowly been culled over the years, or been left behind, singly, in washing machines across Europe and the United States of America. And neither sock matches another odd black sock that sits lonely and de-twinned in the drawer. So I throw away that one instead, even though it looks in much better condition than the dreary nearly-pair whose future I'm now contemplating.

I could so easily shove the black pair to the side and grab a coloured pair instead. It's what I usually do. I even have a sock rotation system going; something I never imagined I would ever share in public, but now the whole sock thing is out in the open I may as well come clean about it. Freshly-laundered socks join my sock pile on the left and I take them from the right. Simple as that. Sometimes this presents me with a sartorial challenge: I've already put on a red t-shirt and the next pair of socks in the queue is also red. Too much. I skip the red socks and take the next pair in line. Come off it, red t-shirt AND red socks? That would be weird, a bit too Butlins, surely? And to those who argue I could lay everything out first rather than have the t-shirt rule the roost, you clearly have no idea how I pick a t-shirt in the morning. It's very simple. Top of the pile wins the day.

I impulsively decide to wear the grey-black socks. Why the fuck not? I'm not wearing a grey-black t-shirt. And even if I were, and it's quite possible I could be, at least I wouldn't look like the director of a summer holiday camp in the red-t-shirt-red-socks combo.

But as I pull the blackish socks effortfully on I can't stop thinking about their history. Or more pressing on my mind, how I've glided from being the man who often needed to pack and wear these quasi-formal socks, to the man who no longer needs them and who might as well throw them away.

Let's face it, these career socks have become metaphor socks. Which are not socks you would usually expect to find in Value Packs of Five on the shelves of Marks & Spencer.

Which brings me to the woman in the bar, Mary.

We've just met Mary, introduced by mutual friends. I'm not aware she is wearing socks when we meet. Unlikely, as it's a hot August evening in Chicago.

We're sitting outside a small bar right next to Lake Michigan, six of us, chatting away, the usual background stuff, where we're from, how we all met. And at small pause, Mary turns to me and asks "So, Chris, where do you usually sing?" A perfectly innocent, polite question, and one I've been asked many times before. And always I take a deep breath, as I do now, wave a hand and say "oh you know, wherever they'll take me."

Only tonight I feel, for some reason, that this will not do. So I start to name some places. And the more I dig into my memory for places Mary may have heard of, the more I cannot recollect where I've sung. I'm suddenly flustered and out-of-sorts. And I become sullen and withdrawn, as if I was presented with a test and failed it, the test being: "Are you successful enough for me to be impressed?" Actors get this all the time. For them the question is "will I have seen you in anything?" And tonight it suddenly and relentlessly triggers an existential crisis.

We were having a lovely time. Why did someone have to go and bring up singing? If I were a dentist, would someone ask me if I had any famous patients? I'm on holiday. Why do I have to be defined by what I do rather than by who I am? There, right there, is the very definition of an existential dilemma. And, particularly, as I stutter towards retirement, singing less and less, do I cease to exist, to matter, to be interesting, simply because I no longer am A Singer? Without that novelty value, what worth am I?

Of course Mary would say don't be silly, she didn't mean to trigger this awful conversation in my head. She was merely being polite and curious. And no doubt the same problem arises for sports-people, particularly those who never made the top rank. Do they become known as ex-sports-people? How many pubs have a bloke pulling pints who used to be a defender for Swindon Town FC. Are those men bartenders or ex-footballers?

And so, thanks to Mary (but no blame assigned to her), a few days of introspection begin, particularly in the middle of the night or in the shower. Yet another re-examination of that thing called *My Career And Why Didn't I Do Better*?"

Well, I won't bore you with all that. Eugh. I imagine every single singer on the planet comes face-to-face with that inner conversation, no matter how much they declare on social media how "lucky and blessed" they are.

"Every single singer on the planet?" I hear you quibble. Yes. We all, every single one of us, face the wall we cannot pass through, the note we cannot sing, the role we cannot perform. Every single singer has the performance they'd rather forget, the disappointment they cannot overcome.

I was once having a post-show pint with Placido Domingo in Los Angeles, in the bar below the Dorothy Chandler Pavilion. He'd been conducting and I'd been singing Basilio in *Le Nozze di Figaro.* When I say "having a pint", this only happened the one time and it's not as if we were the only people in the bar. And I'm not sure if he was even having a beer. I was in the bar. He was in the bar. He was, unusually and briefly, on his own and I was standing nearby. I felt I should strike up a conversation, seeing as we were working together and all, and despite feeling flummoxed by his fame.

"Am I right in remembering you once recorded Basilio's aria?" I said. Boom, straight in with the witty repartee.

"Yes I did, on a disc of Mozart arias. I was supposed to record Tito's aria but I found I couldn't sing it, so I did Basilio instead."

You see? Straight from the horse's mouth: *I COULDN'T SING IT.*

I think I said "Wow!" and nodded my head or something equally stupid and, unsurprisingly, Domingo caught somebody's eye across the bar and disappeared in their direction, clutching the beer he might have had in his hand. And that was it.

Placido Domingo, the man who was sung all the great tenor roles, and a bunch of baritone ones too. Domingo, whom many accuse of not knowing his limitations, admitting his limitations. Imagine having *his* voice and yet not being able to sing everything you might love. Imagine being possessed of a voice of a generation and yet still having constraints on the repertoire you get to do. Did Domingo ever want to sing Bach, Britten? Imagine getting through a tenor career and never singing Haydn's *The Creation, War Requiem, The Saint Matthew Passion...* I certainly can't. And of course we are cut from completely different tenorial cloth. But what of other, heavier roles? Did Domingo ever look at the fearsome role of Siegfried? I can't imagine he did. And Tristan is a role he recorded but never sang on stage.

I doubt Domingo has sleepless nights having *My Career And Why Didn't I Do Better* conversations in his head, and I'm not trying to diss him, but clearly something, some constant urge to prove something, to win some sort of prize, is driving him on into his eighties, when most of us would be lathering Voltarol on our dodgy back and settling down on a squidgy sofa to watch *Midsomer Murders* all afternoon.

Domingo's catchphrase is "If I rest, I rust". Is that really it? Or is he too worried about his own existential crisis? It's a conversation I'd love to have with him over a pint.

Somewhere on YouTube there's a long and strange documentary in which a man called Stefan Zucker ("the world's highest tenor") visits a large number of retired Italian divas. It's a glimpse into the bizarre world of opera fanaticism, a religion whose devotees think that the only good opera performances happened in the past. Zucker - the possessor of a weird falsetto speaking voice and the most horrific singing voice never to have appeared on an actual opera stage, for which we can all be thankful - interviews the old dears about singing. While opera nerds may coo and burble about what they have to say, the ladies themselves make me feel incredibly sad. They live in gloomy apartments with once-opulent furniture. Their pianos, probably now out-of-tune, are laden with photos of themselves with other opera singers - now also incredibly old - taken in the wings of the so-called great houses of the world. An old TV sits in the corner - *Midsomer Murders* is on at 4, the Voltarol is hidden in the bathroom cabinet - and tatty rugs attempt to disguise the ugliness of the beige-tiled floor. These divas are done, over with, only of interest to a handful of bel canto nutters asking them tedious questions about chest voice and *imposto*. Yet when the TV cameras start running they're back in their Sunday best, big hair, plenty of slap, the lot, and sitting bolt upright in their chairs, bolstered not by soft cushions but by big piles of attitude. They just don't like the way things are done anymore.

Well, I want none of that. If anyone comes knocking at my door when I'm done they'll get a swift *fuck-off-I'm-watching-Midsomer-Murders* from me. And it won't be the Voltarol talking.

Stroopwaffel

Amsterdam 2018

I have never, ever been this nervous. And I don't even have to sing. Thank God for that. I don't think I could. Some reflex, memories of the past, a knee-jerk response, had me starting to warm up in the dressing-room until I realised I didn't have to. I was wasting my time. Not that it made me feel any better. I actually feel sick. I don't think I've ever felt sick with nerves before.

What's wrong with me? I'm sixty for christ's sake. I've been performing on this stage for thirty years. But rather than that being a comfort, it's like it's all coming back to haunt me, to swamp me with memories just when I need to focus on what I'm about to do. Three decades of sweaty palms and sweaty soles - I've rarely got to wear shoes on this stage - and three decades of not knowing whether to sit or stand in the wings before I have to go on. And here I am again. Sweaty palms and sweaty soles. Still no shoes.

The wings of the Muziektheater are impressive. There's bags of room. Not like Rome, say, where you have to fight your way through a thirty-inch wide corridor of heaving, chatting Italians before you can make an entrance. No chairs in those wings. Here in Amsterdam, there's plenty of room for chairs. You just have to hope they're not filled up with stage crew.

There are empty chairs tonight. So I sit. Then I stand. Then I sit down again. I burp. I fart. Nothing has changed in that department in the course of my so-called career. Nerves still do funny things to my insides.

Ah, I know what it is.

It feels like this could be the very last time I wait in these wings to run onto that stage.

It's a rather special occasion, a gala to say farewell to Pierre Audi after his thirty years as the artistic director of Dutch National Opera. That's an impressive amount of time spent in one place. Unheard of in the modern opera world. I was in his very first production for the company, *Il Ritorno d'Ulisse in Patria*, and now here I am saying goodbye. The last man standing, it seems.

The place is packed to the hilt, not with the paying public but with invited guests and red carpet types. Ex-Queen Beatrix is in the audience, next to Pierre. There are loads of government ministers, arts honchos and intendants from across the operatic globe. Starry conductors and singers are doing their party pieces. Christof Loy has been called in to direct various chunks. It's a glittering occasion. And this is when I'm going to go on stage and do a short sketch I've written in which I not only lampoon Pierre's directorial style, but impersonate the man himself - something he has never heard me do. I'm about to take the piss out of one of my most loyal employers and friends in front of sixteen hundred people. I've been asked if Pierre has a sense of humour. I said yes. I hope he really does.

It wasn't my idea. Months ago, the house's long-standing *dramaturg*, Klaus Bertisch, emailed saying my impersonation of Pierre was notorious amongst the Dutch Opera staff; would I do it at the gala in some shape or form? Golly.

Now it's one thing to share a joke about Pierre's idiomatic speech over a coffee in the canteen, to whip out the odd catch-phrase in a "funny" voice, but to do it in public, in front of him? When he's sitting next to an ex-queen? It would be mad, possibly career suicide.

I discussed it with my agent. I could hear him squirming with anxiety down the phone line. He really worried it might be a bad idea.

So I said yes. Risky or not, how could I pass up the opportunity for a lovely weekend in Amsterdam, to take part in such a glitzy event?

My first idea was to do a full impersonation of Pierre, to come on dressed as him (always a suit with a chinese collar) complete with elaborate make-up, and do a short routine as Pierre. But I decided it would be terrible. What if, on the night, in the considerable heat of the moment, I couldn't conjure up his voice? I'd just be an idiot in a posh suit just being an idiot. It would be awful and insulting. And not at all funny.

My next inspiration was to come on as me and describe the process of working with Pierre while occasionally using his voice to give me directions. It would be a bit like working with a non-existent ventriloquist's dummy. I'd say something and then "Pierre" would correct me, or tell me I was too close to a wall or something.

It was a better idea, tough to pull off, but I still worried about failing when doing Pierre. His voice is lower than mine. It resonates in a different way. What if I was feeling particularly tenor-y on the day of the gig, or if I had a bit of a cold? I wouldn't be able to do his voice at all and again, it would be awful.

Finally I hit on the answer. I could pre-record me as Pierre giving direction to me as Me. It would be as if he were in the stalls, in the dark, on the "God" mike - the microphone that directors use while they direct shows, that makes their voice boom throughout the theatre - and meanwhile I'd be the hapless singer on stage getting everything a bit wrong so that I as Pierre could correct it in his inimitable way. But not too inimitable. It would all be a matter of timing my moves to a soundtrack I had already prepared.

I wrote a script and sent it to Amsterdam. I had to invent only a few lines for "Pierre" as most of it could be constructed from things I had actually heard the real Pierre say. All I really had to do was to work out what we were pretending to rehearse, and how I as Me was going to move about on stage.

Then I realised that the audience wouldn't have to know what exactly we were rehearsing. I could come on, take a load of direction to get into a position to sing an aria - all in typical Audi style - and then we could simply cut the aria altogether and work on the exit, and no-one need be the wiser. Brilliant. I could go to Amsterdam, do a gig, and not open my mouth once.

Everything that I needed to say would be on tape. This was turning into my idea of a great job.

I also reckoned I couldn't and shouldn't worry whether or not some of the audience - ex-Queen B in particular - were familiar with Pierre's rehearsal style. I had to do this for those in the know, the veterans of working with Pierre. If the gathered intendants of the opera world couldn't figure out what was happening then that would be their problem. (Much like their attitude, no doubt, to the audiences in their own theatres who have to sit through productions of, for instance, *La Boheme* set on the moon.)

I recorded the script on my mobile phone in our bedroom at home; the best place I could find to replicate the resonance of the Muziektheater's auditorium. It was a bit grumpy-sounding and hurried the first time around, and the director of the show, Monique, asked me to try it again with a more positive tone and slower. Good direction. Well done, Monique.

I recorded it again. The trick really lay in visualising what I (as Me) would be doing in front of me (as Pierre). I also changed the last line, on an impulse, to include the name of the stage manager I had worked with on a few of Pierre's shows, my old friend Rudy. I felt it added a nice rim shot for those who would know him, particularly as there was a Pierre quote that used to circulate the Dutch opera: "Rudy! You're ruining my production!" I had no idea if Rudy would be at the gala - I had completely lost touch with him - but I had a hunch there would be at least a few people in the audience who remembered him and would get the gag.

I sent in the new version and Monique was happy. We were good to go.

During the next two weeks I pushed our sitting-room furniture aside and practised my exact moves while listening to the recording of me-as-Pierre over headphones, substituting a length of old copper water pipe for a pole. (All Audi productions have poles. To not have one would be unconscionable.) Given the enormity of the stage in Amsterdam, especially compared to our cosy sitting room, this meant a lot of walking on the spot and even more avoiding knocking over a lamp with a length of copper pipe. Two days before the gala, I flew into Amsterdam (without the copper pipe) and had a few secret rehearsals with Monique. The idea was that none of the audience, especially Pierre, would have any idea who would be performing. Printed programmes would only be available after the show as souvenirs, each number in the gala a surprise for Pierre, for the ex-queen, and for the audience.

It was around the moment I was being told this that I started to have qualms. Massive qualms. I'm not sure how big a qualm can get, but mine were swelling to the size of a five-bedroom house. What if Pierre didn't find it funny? Worse, what if he felt I was belittling thirty years of his work?

I have form with this. I once wrote a very short article about the director Richard Jones which the few people who read it thought was charming and endearing. Except Richard himself who hated it. In the piece I drew attention to some recurring themes in his work - "tropes" if you like. More significantly, I said in the article that some opera fans had latched onto these tropes and that they play what they call Richard Jones Bingo whenever he does a new production. I had honestly thought that Richard, with his inclination to self-deprecation, would find this funny. He didn't. I had made a terrible misjudgment. Was I about to do exactly the same thing to Pierre?

And what about the audience? What if it really were full of stuffed suits and there wasn't one person who has been in a rehearsal room with Pierre? My whole skit could go down like *Springtime For Hitler* in *The Producers*. I could imagine them, sixteen hundred people, their eyes popping and their mouths gaping in horror as I defecated on a man's career and committed professional *harakiri* right in front of them.

So it was no wonder I had started to feel nervous.

--

Walking to the theatre before the show I see a familiar figure just ahead of me. Incredibly, it is Rudy, the ex-stage manager. He's with his new boss, Waut, the intendant of Opera Zuid whom I've never met before.

"I can't tell you how glad I am to see you!" I tell Rudy. "And I can't tell you what it is, but you have a special little treat in store." We promise to meet up at the party afterwards and I head to the stage door. At least there'll be somebody in the audience who gets my sketch. I'm still incredibly nervous though, still sick with anxiety. And an hour later I'm in the wings, waiting for Sandrine Piau to finish her beautiful account of Handel's *Piangero* before I launch myself on stage and make a complete arse of myself.

Applause.

Then a silence while the curtain goes up on an empty, black stage, lit from one side in a single, vivid strip. All very Jean Kalman.

A young stage manager waits with uplifted finger next to me. I hear a murmur into her headset. "Go!" she whispers.

CHRIS enters, in a grey, baggy linen costume, barefoot, holding a long wooden pole. He movers to Centre Stage. Peers into auditorium.

> PIERRE (ON GOD MIKE):
>
> Hello, Chris, how are you?

Chris draws breath to reply but before can speak...

> PIERRE:
>
> OK, let's do the aria, Chris. When you come in, make sure you come in at a slight angle, but do not be too close the wall. It's very important, you see... for the motorique.

Chris nods

> PIERRE:
>
> Show me the position for the aria.

Chris walks over towards stage right. As he walks:

> PIERRE:
>
> Not in a straight line, Chris! It is ugly!

Stops. Assumes a conventional position, holding the pole.

PIERRE:

No, Chris, it is not what we agreed. Turn your body slightly.

Chris starts to turn to his right.

PIERRE:

Not that way, the OTHER way.

Chris turns to his left.

PIERRE:

Closer to the wall.

Chris moves backwards.

PIERRE:

Closer. You have to be five centimeters closer to the wall.

Chris turns his head to gauge the distance to the wall

PIERRE:

But you cannot move your head like that! It is not possible!

Chris takes a tiny step backwards

PIERRE:

No that is too close. You have to be close to the wall but not quite so close. Do you know what I mean?

Chris nods

PIERRE:

Try crouching lower.

Chris crouches a bit

PIERRE:

Lower

Chris ends up down on one knee.

PIERRE:

And delegate more responsibility to your pole, Chris. The pole has to be at right angles to the stage.

Chris adjusts the pole, but doesn't know to which axis the pole has to be at right angles. He tries the front.

PIERRE:

No, Chris, at right angles.

Chris turns the pole through 90 degrees so it is upright.

PIERRE:

The other right angle!

Chris moves the pole again through another 90 degrees.

PIERRE:

Now turn your head. Not that way, the other way. In one movement. Tchack! And try putting your hand forward to the front. We have to feel your inward energy in an outward sort of way.

Chris is now twisted and contorted into an almost impossible position.

PIERRE:

That's it! This is the position for the aria. It is more beautiful, you know?

Chris holds the position, in expectation of singing. Long pause.

PIERRE:

But I'm sorry we do not have time to do the aria now, we just need to do the exit.

So you turn...

Chris rises and starts to turn anti-clockwise

PIERRE:

Not that way, the OTHER way!

Chris turns clockwise.

PIERRE:

And you go off upstage...

Chris heads straight upstage.

PIERRE:

to the other side...

Chris changes direction

PIERRE:

but turn in the middle...

Chris turns

PIERRE:

not that way, the other way...

Chris turns the other way

PIERRE:

in a straight line... but with an angle... not too close to the wall... slower... not too slow

Chris is nearly into the wings

PIERRE:

Thank you Chris.

Chris breaks character, pops back on stage, to acknowledge Pierre's thanks.

PIERRE:

Rudy! What's next?

EXIT

They laugh. A lot. Thank fuck. Judging by the laughter there are lots of old lags like Rudy in the crowd.

At the curtain calls, Pierre comes on stage and works his way down the line of performers. When he gets to me I give him a mock shocked expression. He gives me a big hug and says "Chris! You used ALL my words!"

It's a great occasion. I realise that, like Pierre, my time is over at the Dutch National Opera. And it's fine. It's a good way to go out, to say goodbye, inextricably linked with the man who has given me so much work there. I feel serene, happy even.

The last couple of times I've visited Amsterdam I've steered clear of the Muziektheater, thinking that I wouldn't know anyone there anymore. I had thought it had changed. I'd heard it had, and no doubt it will with someone new in charge. But this weekend was full of old friends, all of us eyeing our retirement, all of us aware you can't keep doing this forever.

When the changes do come, someone else can live with them. It just won't be me. I'll miss the Netherlands as I've loved it so much, but these things have a natural end. And this is mine.

--

A couple of weeks later I get an email from Rudy. They're doing *A Midsummer Night's Dream* at Opera Zuid in 2020. Probably fifteen performances on tour, starting in Maastricht, including one at the Concertgebouw. His boss Waut loved my Pierre sketch. Would I be interested in doing Flute?

"Flute? I'll be sixty-two!"

I thought I was done with Flute.

"Are you sure?"

"Yes, Flute. We think you'll be perfect."

Maastricht is a beautiful town. Good food.
I tell him I'd love to. Now I just need to find out who's my Bottom.

Printed in Great Britain
by Amazon

47579516R00123